CRICKET
Manual

The Haynes *Cricket Manual* is officially licensed by the England and Wales Cricket Board Limited.

Published in June 2009

A catalogue record for this book is available from the British Library

ISBN 978 1 84425 695 2

Library of Congress catalog card no 2009923213

Haynes Publishing,
Sparkford, Yeovil, Somerset BA22 7JJ, UK
Tel: +44 (0) 1963 442030
Fax: +44 (0) 1963 440001
E-mail: sales@haynes.co.uk
Website: www.haynes.co.uk

Haynes North America, Inc.,
861 Lawrence Drive, Newbury Park,
California 91320, USA

Printed and bound in the UK

Editorial Director Mark Hughes

Design Lee Parsons

Photography Getty Images

Author's acknowledgements

Thanks to:

Mhairi and Elizabeth Summers; Jamie and Hannah Tennant; Mark Hughes, Iain Wakefield and Lee Parsons at Haynes; David Hays at Cricket Scotland; everyone who gave their time at ECB including Kelly Hennessy and Kim Parker; ECB Coach Education Department; Tom Keeley at Living with Legends; Jason Ratcliffe at the Professional Cricketers' Association; Michael Vaughan.

CRICKET
Manual

THE OFFICIAL GUIDE TO PLAYING THE GAME

Andy Tennant
Foreword by Michael Vaughan

CONTENTS

FOREWORD

Cricket is undoubtedly the world's finest game. No other sport can provide the tremendous highs and lows that cricket does. The measurable nature of the game and the individual battles that the game provides within a team context are truly unique.

Cricket also has many deeper qualities and a unique spirit that make it a wonderful game to play no matter what level you are competing at. It can also sometimes seem a little complicated to the uninitiated, and one of the aims of the Haynes *Cricket Manual* is to demystify and make sense of some of the game's finer points for anyone who has an interest in cricket.

As a young player I was always looking for ways to learn more about cricket and striving to improve my game in any way that I could. The Haynes *Cricket Manual* is designed to help enthusiasts young and old to learn about the many different aspects of the game, including batting, bowling, fielding, wicketkeeping, captaincy and coaching. It also gives a unique behind-the-scenes look at the National Cricket Performance Centre at Loughborough.

The game of cricket has changed significantly in recent times with the growth of one-day cricket and the emergence of Twenty 20 cricket as an exciting new format along with the continued development of test-match cricket.

The Haynes *Cricket Manual* recognises and promotes a modern approach to developing players while respecting the great traditions and integrity of this wonderful game. It is a 'must read' for all aspiring young cricketers who are striving, as I did, to make the most of their talent.

I hope that all who read the Haynes *Cricket Manual* are inspired to become more involved and passionate about the great game of cricket, and are lucky enough to get as much enjoyment and fulfilment from the game as I have.

Michael Vaughan
Former England Captain

UNDERSTANDING THE GAME

1

CRICKET IN THE 21ST CENTURY

Lord's cricket ground hosts a flood-lit Twenty 20 match

The game of cricket is truly a modern-day sporting chameleon. In its many different guises it has become all things to all men (and women). It is hard to know what a spectator from a hundred years ago would think if they could see a modern English county ground on a Friday evening in June. They would be watching two teams of athletes in coloured clothing playing with a white ball under floodlights in front of packed stands with all the razzmatazz of American Football. They could be forgiven for thinking they were watching a different sport.

In contrast, the game that is still played on sleepy village greens on lazy summer afternoons, between two sets of white-flannelled gentlemen of varying shapes and sizes, would appear to be a throwback to the more gentle-paced era of our time-travelling spectator. Little would appear to have changed from the game they knew. Yet although cricket has become a sport synonymous with tradition, it has always managed to evolve and adapt to its market. Cricket in the 21st century is a testament to that.

The Ashes series of 2005 between England and Australia was a case in point, where test-match cricket – the traditional longer format of the game played over five days – provided some of the most gripping modern-day sporting theatre ever seen. This classic series provided the inspiration for many children to take up the sport, with the England and Wales Cricket Board reporting a 27 per cent increase in participation since then.

ENGLAND
CRICKET

But it is not only in England that the game is growing in popularity. There are now over 100 countries across the world where cricket is played, from the Alps of Austria to the pampas of Argentina and from the lakes of Finland to the islands of Fiji. This is mainly thanks to the global development initiatives run by the International Cricket Council. The ICC is the world governing body for cricket and is committed to promoting and protecting the game.

The globalisation of cricket has gathered pace significantly over the past ten years and there is likely now to be a period of consolidation, to raise the standard and infrastructure for cricket in many of these fledgling regions. The impact of globalisation is also being seen at the top level, however, and few cricket fans will forget the performance of the Kenyan team at the ICC World Cup in South Africa in 2003, or Ireland's dramatic win over Pakistan in Jamaica during the 2007 World Cup. These achievements would have been unthinkable until recently, but show just how the traditional powerhouses of world cricket are being challenged from the most unlikely of sources.

In addition to the game's rapid spread across the globe, the amount of money flooding in is also changing the face of cricket. Just as the advent of one-day cricket revolutionised the game in the 1960s and '70s, Twenty 20 cricket is the latest format to take the world by storm. This new phenomenon has become incredibly popular with players, spectators and sponsors alike. The relatively short time that a match takes to complete seems to fit well with these fast-paced times and the busy lives that people lead today. As a result the game at professional level is filling stadiums, attracting sponsors and wooing TV companies, and the revenue that it can generate has increased significantly. The ICC has recently negotiated a seven-year global TV deal worth in excess of a billion dollars for all its events. This shows the huge popularity and appeal of cricket, particularly on the Indian sub-continent, and the revenue will help to sustain and develop the game for many years to come.

The rise in popularity of the Twenty 20 format has also led to many new competitions promoting this latest form of the game, and the Indian Premier League (IPL) has played its part in increasing the profile of the game. But while the influx of money provided by such events is welcome, it is important that their staging and regularity is managed carefully for the long-term benefit of the sport. The many varying formats of the game that now exist have created a very fragile 'eco-system' that needs to be protected, and their careful management is probably the biggest challenge facing

modern cricket. As the classic fable points out, it is important not to kill the goose that lays the golden egg.

Another development that has shaped the ongoing development of cricket has been the rise in popularity of the women's game. For two centuries cricket had been a traditionally male preserve with only a few notable exceptions, but today the women's game at international level – particularly in its shorter forms – is going from strength to strength, with worldwide development initiatives attracting many new players. The ICC Women's Cricket World Cup in Australia in 2009 was the largest women's event ever staged, with a worldwide TV audience of millions. This augurs well not only for the women's game but for the sport in general.

So much has changed in such a short space of time that it is a wonder cricket has retained so much of its charm. Hopefully the next section will help explain how it has managed to.

England's Andrew Flintoff playing for Chennai Super Kings in the Indian Premier League (IPL)

The true origins of cricket are lost in the mists of time, but the majority view is that the game was first played in the Weald, an area of south-east England that covers parts of Kent and Sussex. It is believed that it may have originated as a game played principally by children on grazed farmland. A stick or staff was used to prevent a ball of tightly wrapped sheep's wool or sometimes a stone from hitting a stool or gate. This gate was sometimes a 'wicket gate', which had a horizontal wooden stick set upon two wooden uprights – the original form of wicket prior to the third or middle stump being introduced in the late 18th century.

The name 'cricket' may have come from the old English word for a staff (*cricc*), and the earliest official written reference records *creckett* being played around the middle of the 16th century at the Royal Grammar School at Guildford in Surrey. The game became more popular among adults in the 17th century, with parish and village matches taking place, and gradually cricket became a major gambling sport. This led, through the 18th century, to increased interest from aristocrats and businessmen, who became patrons of chosen teams that were strengthened by selecting the best men available in the county – giving rise to the beginnings of professional county cricket.

The 1760s saw the Hambledon Cricket Club in Hampshire become the first organised centre of cricket in England. They started the first cricketing dynasty, and for many years they were more than a match for all-comers on Broadhalfpenny Down. Hambledon remained the heart of cricket for almost 30 years until the formation of the MCC in London.

The mechanics of the game were also changing, with the traditional rolling of the ball at the wicket being replaced by underarm bowling. These new 'deceitful' bowlers would vary the flight and length of the delivery in an effort to dismiss the batsmen. As a result the traditional bent stick, which looked a bit like an old-fashioned hockey stick, became ineffective and a wider, straighter bat was preferred.

As a result of the high stakes being played for, 'articles of agreement' were drawn up by patrons prior to matches to remove any causes of doubt in the settling of associated gambling debts. This led to the laws of the game first being codified in 1744, before being amended 30 years later to take into account the rapidly evolving techniques being employed. The law 'leg before wicket', for example, was introduced to stop batsmen from deliberately preventing the ball from hitting the wicket by placing their leg in the way. The 1774 amendments were made by the Star and Garter Club, whose members were eventually to form the Marylebone Cricket Club. The MCC, as it has come to be known, remain the custodians of the laws of cricket to this day.

Meanwhile the game was evolving to more closely resemble the sport we know today. Additions such as umpires and a middle stump for the traditional wicket were introduced, followed in the early 1800s by radical innovations such as 'round arm bowling', a forerunner to the overarm technique we know today.

As well as becoming more recognisable as cricket and more regulated, the game was also becoming more popular. It spread north throughout the country to Yorkshire and Scotland, and also spread overseas as British influence across the globe grew and the empire expanded to new territories. It was popularised principally by British soldiers, sailors and administrators, and by the early 1800s was being widely played in India, Australia, New Zealand and South Africa.

The early 19th century also saw the formation of county clubs, with Sussex fittingly being the first. Then in the 1840s the growth of 'first-class' county cricket encountered competition in the form of cricket's first

Cricket being played in about 1740 at the Royal Artillery Ground, London

W.G. Grace,
England's first
cricketing
superstar, 1900

'rebellion', as Nottingham man William Clarke's All-England Eleven played matches principally in the big northern cities. These 'circus'-style matches proved a great financial success and did much to showcase the best players and popularise the game. The MCC and county cricket, however, eventually prevailed, as the growing railway network made travelling easier and inter-county matches more accessible. The demise of the All-England Eleven coincided with the formation of the County Cricket Championship in 1890. This period in the history of the game also saw the legalisation of overarm bowling and the emergence of 'stars' such as W.G. Grace in England and Victor Trumper in Australia.

The first international cricket match had, however, taken place nearly 50 years earlier. Surprisingly the match was not played between England and Australia but between the USA and Canada, at St Georges Park, New York, in the summer of 1844. International cricket took off for real with the first tour of Australia by England in 1877. This tour was reciprocated in 1882 when an Australian team defeated England on English soil for the first time, winning by seven runs at the Oval. This defeat was not taken well in England, the cradle of the game, and a mock obituary to English cricket appeared in the *Sporting Times* newspaper. The satirical piece stated that 'English cricket had died, the body will be cremated and the ashes taken to Australia.' The next tour by England down-under then became popularly known as 'the quest to regain the Ashes', during which the England captain was presented with a small terracotta urn – believed to contain a burnt bail – by a group of Melbourne women. And so the legend was born, with England playing Australia every two years for 'the Ashes'. Many people consider this period, from the late 19th century up to the outbreak of the First World War in 1914, as the sport's 'golden age', and the defining era of the 'spirit of cricket'.

In 1909 came the formation of the Imperial Cricket Conference, which became the first world governing body. The three founding member nations were England, Australia and South Africa; India, New Zealand and the West Indies joined before the Second World War, and Pakistan joined in 1947 following the partition of India. More recently Sri Lanka, Zimbabwe and Bangladesh have joined as full test-playing members of what is now called the International Cricket Council, which has 10 full members, 34 associate members and 60 affiliates.

The 20th century featured several controversies, including the distasteful 'bodyline' series of the 1930s when England's ruthless tactics in combating the dominant Australians stretched the spirit of the game and international relations to breaking point. In the 1970s Kerry Packer's rebel 'World Series' Cricket challenged the authority of the cricketing establishment, and during the 1990s there were match-fixing scandals that rocked cricket in both Asia and South Africa and had repercussions throughout the cricketing world, with several leading players being banned for life.

The latter part of the century also saw the advent of one-day cricket, which, like many changes over the years, allowed the game to evolve and adapt to changing times. One-day cricket was a reaction to the dull county cricket being played in England in the 1960s, with scoring rates dropping to little more than two runs an over. In an effort to produce more entertaining games and improve scoring rates, the 60-overs-a-side Gillette Cup became the first domestic one-day competition in 1963. The first 'limited-overs' internationals took place in the early '70s and the first Cricket World Cup took place in England in 1975. This led in turn to One-Day Internationals (ODIs), which with a standardised 50-overs-a-side format has become the most popular form of the game in many parts of the world. The 50-overs format has more recently been superseded by a new phenomenon called Twenty 20, a 20-overs-a-side form of the game that has recently swept the globe.

THE SPIRIT OF CRICKET

Andrew Flintoff shakes the hand of Australia's Brett Lee in consolation following England's victory by two runs at Edgbaston during the memorable Ashes series of 2005

An awareness of the spirit of cricket seems to have emerged during the sport's 'golden era' in the late 19th and early 20th centuries. Victorian Britain had a keen sense of the 'positive impact' of the Empire and the notion of 'British values' of honesty, integrity and fair play. These values were seen at the time as being played out on the cricket field, and led to an appreciation of the unique spirit of the game.

Though the cold light of post-colonial times may now give us a different perspective of the rights and wrongs of the Empire, there can be no doubt that this nostalgic view did exist at the time, especially in the dark days following the Great War, which had wiped out a generation of young men. There is also no doubt that cricket has become synonymous with fair play,

hence the saying 'it's just not cricket' when an unjust or dishonest event occurs.

Lord Harris wrote a letter to *The Times* in 1931 that epitomised the fondness for the game and the reverence in which cricket was held in the period between the wars:

'You do well to love it, for it is more free from anything sordid, anything dishonourable, than any game in the world. To play it keenly, honourably, generously, self-sacrificingly, is a moral lesson in itself, and the classroom is God's air and sunshine. Foster it my brothers so that it may attract all who can find time to play it; protect it from anything that would sully it, so that it may grow in favour with all men.'

Lord Harris's appeal to protect the game and maintain its unique set of standards has been revitalised in recent years by two former England captains, Ted Dexter and Lord Cowdrey. They championed an initiative that led to a preamble on the spirit of cricket being added to the laws in the latest revision in 2000. It begins:

'Cricket is a game that owes much of its unique appeal to the fact that it should be played not only within its Laws but also within the Spirit of the Game. Any action which is seen to abuse this spirit causes injury to the game itself. The major responsibility for ensuring the spirit of fair play rests with the captains'.

This worthy initiative has more recently been supported by the MCC 'Spirit of Cricket' initiative which encourages cricketers young and old to 'Play Hard –

Play Fair'. Although at times it would appear that something of this spirit has been lost in the modern-day game, the vast majority of players still uphold the traditional values that cricket stands for.

There is also a unique sense within cricket that the participants are the custodians of the game. As such each player has a responsibility to uphold the spirit of cricket. Some doubters may dismiss this as a naïve view but it is this very spirit that may well be cricket's great redeeming feature. The education system has certainly shown renewed interest in cricket as a result of the values that it teaches. Recent research also seems to back this up, with an increase in 'good behaviour' being displayed by school pupils who had recently been introduced to cricket. This is in marked contrast to the ill-disciplined behaviour which blights other popular sports.

England fielders offer 'three cheers' for Donald Bradman on the occasion of his final test match at the Oval in 1948

CRICKET'S VARIOUS FORMATS

Test-match cricket: England take the wicket of New Zealand's Brendon McCullum during a test match at Trent Bridge, Nottingham

THE LONGER GAME

TEST MATCHES

The test match is the longest form of the game, with five days' play scheduled to try and obtain a positive result. Matches are played by the national teams of the ICC's full member nations, and ten countries currently play test matches against each other. Test matches are normally played in a series of three to five matches and often incorporated within a longer tour. A tour may also include some one-day internationals, Twenty 20 internationals and first-class matches against the leading domestic teams within the host nation.

Test-match cricket is still seen by most as the pinnacle of the international game and the truest test of a cricketer's skills. Test cricket has now been played for over 130 years, and over this time the biennual 'Ashes' series between England and Australia has become the best-known, although India v Pakistan test matches are the most widely followed and fiercely contested.

All test-match series are now arranged several years in advance through the ICC Future Tours Programme and this has led to the formation of an ICC Test Match Championship. This championship ranks the nations from 1 to 10 in accordance with their results. Australia has been top of the world rankings for all but a few months since their inception in 2001.

ENGLAND
CRICKET

There is also now a recognised test-match structure for women's cricket. The women's game has recently become integrated into the International Cricket Council. One-day internationals do, however, take precedence in the female game.

FIRST-CLASS CRICKET

'First-class cricket' is generally defined as a match of three or more days' duration between two sides within the ten test-playing nations that have been adjudged by the official governing body for cricket to have 'first-class' status.

However, first-class cricket – which technically includes test cricket – is generally accepted to be the highest level of two-innings domestic cricket (normally played by professionals) within the major nations. The national governing body for cricket in each country is responsible for defining which matches are granted first-class status. In order to be recognised these games have to represent the very highest playing standard. Some major two-innings internationals between the leading 'associate' nations have also been granted first-class status. These include matches between Scotland and Ireland and the new four-day Inter-Continental Cup between the eight leading Associate nations.

First-class competitions around the world have become extremely popular and important within their respective countries. The County Championship in England has been in existence since 1890, with Yorkshire and Surrey being the most successful counties statistically, with 30 and 18 titles respectively. In Australia, New South Wales have won their first-class competition, the Sheffield Shield, a record 45 times. Mumbai (formerly Bombay) have won India's Ranji Trophy 37 times.

All first-class cricket, including test matches, is played in the more traditional white clothing and with a red ball, in accordance with the Laws of Cricket.

First-class cricket: Nottinghamshire against Hampshire, 2008 LV County Championship

THE SHORTER GAME
LIMITED OVERS CRICKET

ONE-DAY CRICKET

One-day cricket, as it has come to be known (due to the intention of completing a match within a single day's play), is normally played over 50 overs per side. The highest score wins in limited-overs cricket, thus eliminating the possibility of a draw, although a tied score is still possible. When this form of the game was introduced it was seen as an exciting development which removed the boring draw that a side could claim if the opposing side, though scoring the higher amount of runs, failed to capture all ten of their wickets. Some recreational cricket still plays limited-overs games that retain the traditional draw, but this is becoming much less common.

The first one-day competition in professional cricket was the Gillette Cup, which was established in England in 1963. Limited-overs internationals, as they were known in those days, started in the early 1970s. These were originally played over 60 overs, but most domestic one-day cricket and all one-day internationals are now played over 50 overs, with a standardised format and playing conditions. The pinnacle of the one-day game is the ICC Cricket World Cup, with Australia having won four of the nine that have been contested.

One of the great challenges faced by one-day cricket is deciding a winner in rain-affected matches. After many years of searching for a suitable method, the game would appear to have settled on a system based on statistical analysis devised by the English statisticians and cricketing enthusiasts Duckworth and Lewis. This has now become an accepted international standard.

TWENTY 20 CRICKET

The newest format of the game, 'T20' is a shortened version of one-day cricket, with the intention of completing the match in less than three hours. It has become incredibly popular since its inception in 2003 and is regularly filling cricket stadiums around the world. It seems strange that a format which has been in

Action from a one-day match between Middlesex and Surrey

ENGLAND CRICKET

widespread use in recreational games for decades has become such a phenomenon, but for many years 20-over cricket was considered to be beneath the professional game.

The shorter length of time taken to complete a match seems to appeal to our modern lifestyles. Another important selling point is the fact that matches can be staged in the evening when people have finished work. International Twenty 20 cricket is also now becoming popular, with the inaugural World T20 in South Africa in 2007 having been a huge commercial success.

T20's great commercial appeal has, however, created great challenges for the game's administrators. Its unparalleled popularity has put the game's best players in great demand, with rival leagues competing for their services. Competitions like the Indian Premier League are now being replicated the world over, and careful management of the best players' fixture programmes will be required if the game's current global harmony is to be maintained.

All limited-overs cricket in the professional game is now played in coloured clothing with a white ball, thus clearly distinguishing it from the first-class game. Limited-overs matches are played according to the laws of cricket but with amended playing conditions that are designed to benefit their intended free-scoring nature. Many matches are now completed under floodlights with day/night one-day cricket matches in England commencing at 2:00pm. Most T20 matches in England commence around 5:00pm, with Friday becoming an increasingly popular evening for them.

OTHER FORMS OF CRICKET

There are many other formats of the game which have been adapted to allow people in different environments to enjoy the contest between bat and ball. Modified small-sided games such as 'kwik cricket' and inter-cricket are played to help children learn how to play. Indoor and beach cricket are principally recreational forms of the game suited to their specific environments. Other variations include 'Tapeball', which is very popular in the Indian sub-continent and is played in the streets or parks using a taped-up tennis ball.

DISABILITY CRICKET

Disability cricket is a growing area for the sport in the UK and the England and Wales Cricket Board (ECB) are generally regarded as the world's leading governing body in the development of cricket for people with a disability.

There are various different categories of disability cricket. These include deaf cricket for people with hearing impairments, blind cricket for the visually impaired (with sub-categories depending on the degree of impairment), and cricket for people with learning difficulties. There are England performance squads competing on the international stage in these three forms of the disability game as well as regional and recreational opportunities for people with a physical disability.

Table cricket is also a popular form of the game for cricket lovers with a disability.

All this clearly shows that nowadays there are many opportunities for people with a disability to become involved in cricket. The ECB also now have a national disabilities manager and anyone who is interested in becoming involved in this form of the game should e-mail the ECB at: *disabilitycricket@ecb.co.uk*

Chris Foster bowls for an ECB Physically Disabled XI

WOMEN'S CRICKET

England celebrate winning the ICC Women's World Cup in Sydney, March 2009

The women's game has developed significantly in the past ten years in both the UK (since the Women's Cricket Association became part of the ECB) and on a global scale (since the ICC took over the administration and development of cricket for women as well as men).

This has led to a significant increase in the profile of women's cricket. Thich culminated in the 2009 ICC Women's Cricket World Cup being the highest-profile women's cricket tournament ever staged. The Trophy was won by England who defeated the New Zealand 'White Ferns' in the Final. The profile of the game was further enhanced in March 2009 when England's star batter, Claire Taylor, was unveiled as one of the 'five cricketers of the year' by Wisden. This was the first time a female cricketer had been recognised by cricket's most prestigious individual award.

This dramatic increase in the profile of the women's game, coupled with outstanding grass-roots development work over the past decade, has led to a sharp rise in the number of girls taking up the game. In 2007 alone there was a 45 per cent increase in the number of girls playing cricket in England and Wales. Although girls have had the opportunity to try cricket through 'kwik cricket' and other modified forms of the game for many years, it is only recently that many clubs have started to offer girls the opportunity to play the game with and against their female peers. This has led to a massive increase in the number of competitions and

opportunities for girls and women to play cricket, and further significant growth is predicted in the future.

The basic principles for the development of male and female cricketers are to all intents and purposes the same and the content of this manual holds true for all cricketers. It is important to note that the physical differences between male and female participants following maturation lead to differences in the way that technical, tactical and physical skills are developed. While the women's game may not always feature the same speed and power as the men's game, the development of technical excellence and heightened tactical awareness can make the women's game equally compelling.

Claire Taylor pictured in the Long Room at Lord's after becoming a Wisden Cricketer of the Year

Taunton Cricket Ground became the 'official home' of English women's cricket in 2006

THE CRICKET PITCH

England coaches Peter Moores and Andy Flower discuss the wicket at Chester-le-Street with the groundsman

Shown on the facing page is an isometric view of a cricket pitch, or wicket as it is more commonly known. The wicket is normally 22yds (20.1m) long, cut from a 10ft (3.05m) wide strip that is pre-prepared by watering, rolling and protecting from the elements. The pitch or wicket is part of a larger prepared rectangular area in the centre of the ground known as the 'square'.

How the wicket will play is dependent on how the pitch has been prepared prior to the match.

Under-prepared pitches that have not been rolled sufficiently, or pitches that are damp, are known as 'green' wickets and tend to favour the bowlers, particularly faster bowlers. This is due to the unpredictable way in which the ball may behave when hitting the pitch, thus making it far harder for the batter to hit it consistently.

Wickets that are straw-coloured with an even grass covering, that have been prepared in ideal conditions and have been given an optimal amount of watering and rolling tend to play in a true and predictable way. This traditionally favours the batters, who can better predict the bounce of the ball and successfully execute their chosen shot.

Pitches that are very dry with a less-than-even grass covering can sometimes become unpredictable in the way the ball bounces and deviates off the pitch. This again makes it harder for the batters. This type of pitch tends to favour the spin bowlers, who can deceive the batters with unpredictable bounce and lateral movement. This is created by the amount of spin they impart on the ball when delivering it towards the batter.

These pitches are sometimes referred to as 'dustbowls'.

The choice of who bats first in every match is decided by the toss of a coin between the two captains. Judging how the pitch is likely to play throughout the course of the match is key for the captain who wins the toss. The correct assessment of favourable conditions will influence whether the captain decides to bat or field first and can have a significant bearing on the outcome of the match.

Pitches in different parts of the world tend to play in different ways, mainly due to climate and other related factors. As a result certain parts of the world have gained a reputation for favouring differing styles of play, particularly when related to bowlers. An example would be that in general the Indian sub-continent tends to favour spin bowlers, while Australia and South Africa favour the faster bowlers. Different grounds in the same country also gain a reputation for playing in a certain way and influence how captains, teams and individuals approach the game.

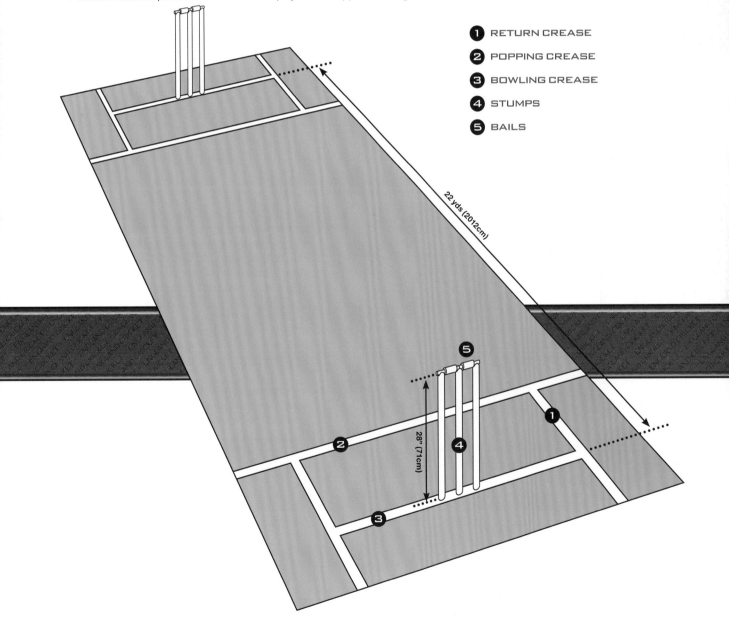

1 RETURN CREASE

2 POPPING CREASE

3 BOWLING CREASE

4 STUMPS

5 BAILS

22 yds (2012cm)

28" (71cm)

BAT

The specifications of a cricket bat are tightly regulated to ensure the contest between bat and ball is a fair one. The bat must be made of wood and is made up of two distinct parts, the handle and the blade. The blade is traditionally made of willow and has a maximum permitted width of 4¼in (108mm). The bat must also be no more than 38in (970mm) high. There is no maximum permitted weight, but most full-size bats weigh between 2lb 4oz (approximately 1kg) and 3lb (approximately 1.3kg). Smaller bats are also available for shorter adult players and children. In modified forms of the game other materials may be used, such as plastic bats in 'kwik cricket'.

BALL

The traditional cricket ball is a hard leather-covered sphere with a thread-stitched seam. It is normally dark red in colour although a white ball is now used in limited-overs cricket at professional level, where coloured clothing is also worn. The specification of the ball is also tightly regulated within the laws of cricket. They state that the ball for adult male matches must be 5½oz (156gm). The ball in women's cricket is normally 5oz (142gm) and in children's cricket it is 4¾oz (135gm). As with the bat, in less formal and modified forms of the game other types of ball are used, such as a tennis ball or plastic ball in 'kwik cricket'.

**An experimental pink ball
used in the MCC v Scotland
match at Lord's in April 2008**

FIELDING POSITIONS

In any match one team of 11 players will be in the field. One player will be bowling and one, with gloves on, will be keeping wicket behind the batter and the stumps. This leaves nine fielders who are strategically placed by the captain. This is normally done in consultation with the bowler. The aim is to place a fielder in the best position to catch the ball in order to dismiss the batter, or to field the ball on the ground to prevent runs being scored and/or to run the batter out.

The fielding positions are very flexible, as shown below, and there are many variations on a single fielding position. The names of the positions can sometimes seem obscure but are part of the game's great traditions. The bowler and captain can place fielders almost anywhere, with a few notable exceptions. There will, however, always be many gaps for the ball to be hit into and the speed and agility of fielders is crucial in restricting the score of the batting team.

Shown below are the key field positions for a right-handed batter, and examples of how they can be varied. For a left-hander, who faces the opposite way, these positions would simply be reversed mirror-fashion.

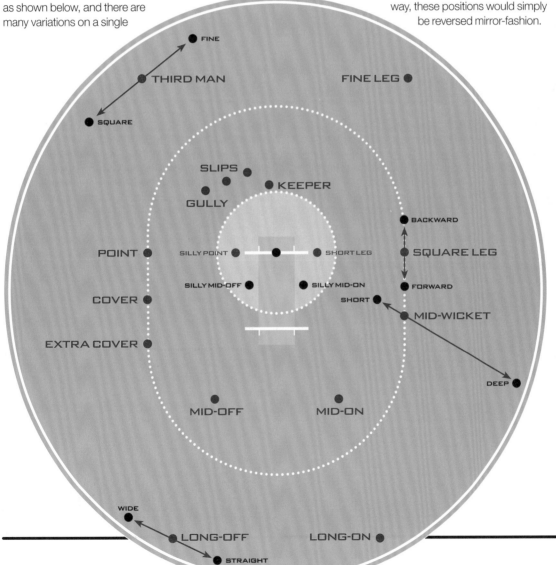

UNDERSTANDING THE LAWS

The laws of cricket were first codified in the 18th century, and for more than 200 years the Marylebone Cricket Club, based at Lord's cricket ground, have been their custodian. Any changes made to the laws are now done in close consultation with the world governing body, the ICC. The most recent changes were made in 2000. Cricket is unique in that it has a set of 42 laws, rather than rules, which govern how the game is played. Variations, known as playing conditions, can, however, be applied to take into account different formats and competitions.

A summary of how the laws are structured and some of the key features are as follows:

LAWS 1–4 refer to the people who play and preside over the game. For example, Laws 1 and 2 relate to the players and substitutes.

■ **Law 1.1** states: 'A match is played between two sides, each of 11 players, one of whom shall be captain. By agreement a match may be played between sides of more or less than 11 players, but not more than 11 players may field at any time.'

■ **Laws 3 and 4** relate to the umpires and scorers appointed to officiate during the match.

■ **Laws 5 to 11** deal with the equipment and the pitch specifications, including the preparation, maintenance and covering of the playing area. Much of the information on pitch specifications is covered in the previous section of this book.

■ **Laws 12 to 17** govern the structure of the game. This includes the agreed number of innings or overs which make up the game, and agreed start and finish times, including intervals.

LAWS 18–29 include the ones that are probably the most important for the players, as they denote how to score runs and take wickets and how the game is won and lost. A summary of each of the most relevant of them is therefore given below (please note, however, that these are simplified explanations, and should not be mistaken for the actual laws as written).

■ **Law 18** (scoring runs): A run is scored when the batters cross and make their ground in the crease at the other end. More than one run may be scored from each delivery.

■ **Law 19** (boundaries): A boundary is scored and signalled by the umpire at the bowler's end when a ball which has been struck by the bat reaches the boundary.

Four runs are scored when the ball reaches the boundary after having bounced or rolled within the field of play. Six runs are scored when the ball reaches beyond the boundary before bouncing. (The rope or line which defines the boundary is deemed to be beyond the boundary.)

■ **Law 21** (the result): The side which scores the most runs wins the match. If the scores are equal at the end of play then the match is normally tied. In matches other than limited-overs matches, where both teams score the same amount of runs the side batting second must have lost all available wickets for the match to be deemed a tie, otherwise the match will be deemed a draw. A draw also occurs in non-limited-overs matches if time runs out before all innings have been completed.

■ **Law 22** (the over): An over consists of a set six balls bowled, excluding 'illegal' deliveries such as no balls and wides. Overs are bowled from alternate ends in sets of six and no bowler may bowl two consecutive overs.

■ **Law 24** (no ball): There are various reasons why a no ball is called. The ball must be bowled with some part of the bowler's front foot (in their delivery stride) behind the front crease line (known as the popping crease), otherwise the umpire at the bowler's end will call a no ball. Similarly the bowler's back foot in their delivery stride must land entirely within the side line of the crease (known as the return crease) otherwise a no ball will be called. Other reasons why a no ball would be called include throwing – when a bowler bends and straightens their arm during the delivery – or when fielders are in a position which contravenes the laws or playing conditions. The penalty for a no ball is one run plus any additional runs scored from the delivery. It is also worth remembering that a no ball is not a legitimate delivery and does not count for one of the six 'legal' deliveries required to complete an over.

■ **Law 25** (wide ball): A ball is called wide if the umpire decides that in their opinion it has passed wide of where the batter is standing and would also have passed wide of their initial position – in other words, the ball is not sufficiently within their reach for them to be able to hit it with their bat by means of a normal cricket stroke.

■ **Law 26** (bye and leg bye): Following a legal delivery which passes the striker without touching their bat or person, any runs completed by the batter (including a boundary) are credited as byes to the batting side. If a ball delivered by the bowler first strikes the batter, runs are scored if the umpire is satisfied that the batter either attempted to hit the ball with their bat or attempted to avoid being hit by the ball. If the ball then makes no subsequent contact with the bat, runs completed by the batter (including a boundary) are credited to the batting side as leg byes.

■ **Laws 27 to 29** relate to the three ways that a batter can be dismissed; these are then covered by the ten methods of dismissal, which are covered in Laws 30 to 39:

■ **Law 27** (appeals): A bowler or fielder may appeal if they believe the batter to be out within the laws of the game. The most common methods of dismissal which require an appeal are LBW (leg before wicket) or caught behind the wicket (where there is an element of doubt as to whether the batter hit the ball). An appeal usually consists of a forceful cry of 'How's that?' Neither umpire will give a batsman out, even though they may be out under the laws, unless appealed to by the fielding side, but this does not debar a batsman who is out from leaving his wicket without an appeal having been made.

■ **Law 28** (the wicket is down): Several methods of dismissal can occur as a result of the wicket being down. The wicket is down if at least one bail is dislodged from the top of the stumps or a stump is struck out of the ground by the ball, the batter, or a member of the fielding team while holding the ball. Bowled is the most obvious method of dismissal in which the wicket is down.

■ **Law 29** (batsman out of his ground): A batter is out of his ground unless the bat or some part of his person is grounded behind the front crease line at that end. Methods of dismissal where batters are out of their ground would include stumped and run out.

LAWS 30 – 39 cover the ten ways in which a batter can be dismissed:

■ **Law 30** (bowled): The batter is bowled if their wicket is 'put down' (ie, a bail is dislodged) by a ball delivered by the bowler (other than a no ball), even if it first touches their bat or person.

■ **Law 31** (timed out): An incoming batter must be ready to face the next ball (or their partner must be ready to face it if appropriate) within three minutes of the fall of the previous wicket. If this requirement is not met the incoming batter will be out.

■ **Law 32** (caught): If a ball delivered by the bowler (other than a no ball) hits the bat or the hand holding the bat, and is then caught and held by a fielder before touching the ground, the batter is out.

■ **Law 33** (handled the ball): Either batter is out if they wilfully touch the ball while in play with a hand or hands not holding the bat, unless they do so with the consent of the opposing side.

■ **Law 34** (hit the ball twice): The batter is out if, while the ball is in play, it strikes any part of their person or is struck by the bat and, before it has been touched by a fielder, they wilfully strike it again, except for the sole purpose of guarding their wicket.

■ **Law 35** (hit wicket): If, after the bowler has entered their delivery stride and while the ball is in play, the striking batter puts their own wicket down with their bat or person, then they are out.

■ **Law 36** (leg before wicket): If, in the umpire's opinion, a ball (other than a no ball) hits the batter either without or before hitting the bat, but would have hit the wicket had the batter not been there, and the ball has not pitched on the leg side of the wicket, the batter will be out. However, if the ball strikes the batter outside the line of the off-stump, and they were attempting to play a stroke, they are not out.

■ **Law 37** (obstructing the field): If either batter wilfully obstructs or distracts the opposing team by either words or actions, they are out. Examples of this would include a batter deliberately preventing a catch or a run-out from being completed.

■ **Law 38** (run out): Except in exceptional circumstances, either batter is out if at any time while the ball is in play they are out of their ground and their wicket is fairly put down by the opposing side.

■ **Law 39** (stumped): The batter is out if, while receiving a ball that is not a no ball, they are out of their ground while not attempting a run and the wicket is fairly put down by the wicketkeeper, without the intervention of another member of the fielding side.

A batter may also be 'retired out' either by himself or his captain. This is not, however, a recognised form of dismissal and is covered within Law 2.9.

■ **Laws 40 and 41** govern the wicketkeeper and the fielders and relate principally to equipment allowed, positioning and movement.

■ **Law 42** (fair and unfair play) states that it is the responsibility of the captains to ensure that play is conducted within the spirit and traditions of the game, and that the umpires are the sole judges of fair and unfair play. Examples of things covered include changing the condition of the match ball, deliberate attempts to distract the batter and dangerous and unfair bowling, to name but a few.

THE OFFICIALS

Legendary umpire Steve Bucknor officiates in his final international match between the West Indies and England

UMPIRES

Two on-field umpires are appointed to control the game with absolute impartiality and according to the laws of cricket. One umpire stands behind the wicket at the bowler's end and the other normally stands at a position called square leg. This is level with the line of the popping crease at the batter's end, close enough to have a clear view but a safe distance away (usually 20–25yds). The umpires swap position at the end of each over while remaining at the same end of the wicket. This allows overs to be bowled alternately from either end.

The umpire at the bowler's end tends to make most of the key decisions including no balls, wides and appeals for leg before wicket and caught behind the

wicket. The square-leg umpire makes decisions mainly on stumpings and run-outs. In more high-profile and televised matches, the on-field umpires may refer decisions to a third 'off-field' umpire who is empowered to make decisions using video evidence. The on-field umpires are also responsible for many other things such as judging fair and unfair play, the fitness of the ground, weather and light for play, signalling decisions and ensuring the correctness of the score in consultation with the scorers.

SCORERS

The details of a cricket match are recorded by the scorers. There are normally two of these, one from each side, to ensure the correct recording of all

ENGLAND
CRICKET

statistics from the match. The scorers watch every ball and record the score. The statistics from each match are generally recorded in an official scorebook. The scorers also respond to a series of coded signals from the umpire which bring clarity to the decisions the umpire has made on the field. The scorers tend to sit in or near the scoreboard, to ensure the information displayed on the board is correct.

The scorers are responsible for recording the total number of runs scored, wickets taken and overs bowled. They also record which individuals score runs, bowl overs, take wickets and make catches. This allows individual statistics for each player to be recorded for each match. The recording of this information is seen as very important and players build up statistical averages to evaluate their performance over a period of time. Scorers therefore play a significant part in the statistical analysis of the game and have become an integral part of cricket's unique culture.

MATCH/TOURNAMENT REFEREE

A referee is appointed in matches at international level, such as test matches and one-day internationals. He is appointed by the ICC and remains off the field during play but is the official observer at the match. His or her job is to ensure that the ICC code of conduct is upheld throughout the match, thus ensuring the maintenance of standards of behaviour to the highest level. The referee does not influence any on-field decisions, which are entirely the responsibility of the appointed umpires. The umpire may, however, refer on-field incidents to the match referee to deal with, such as incidents of player dissent. In certain less high-profile events a tournament referee may be appointed to oversee all matches staged.

Daryl Harper and Monty Panesar share a joke during a test match

UMPIRE'S SIGNALS

During play, the umpire at the bowler's end makes the majority of the decisions. These are indicated to the scorers and spectators by means of a series of coded movements, made mainly with the arms. Most decisions are made and signalled instantaneously but some may be made only after consultation with the square leg and/or third umpire. The agreed code of signals used by umpires is regulated by the laws of cricket. The most frequently used signals are illustrated here.

OUT
Umpire raises his index finger above shoulder level

FOUR
Umpire waves his arm from side to side in front of his body

SIX
Umpire raises both hands above his head

WIDE
Umpire stretches out both arms as wide as possible

NO BALL
Umpire stretches one arm out to the side

ENGLAND
CRICKET

DEAD BALL

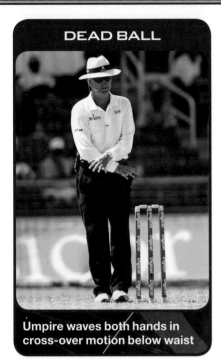

Umpire waves both hands in cross-over motion below waist

BYE

Umpire raises one hand above the head

LEG BYE

Umpire taps hand on outstretched leg

ONE SHORT

Umpire taps one hand on shoulder

There are several other signals that umpires now use, especially in limited-overs cricket:

POWERPLAY
Sections of one-day matches when special fielding restrictions apply.
- Umpire waves one arm vertically in circular motion.

FREE HIT
Following a front-foot no ball in one-day matches, the batter is allowed a free hit.
- Umpire waves one hand in circular motion above head.

REFERRAL TO THIRD UMPIRE
Video evidence can be used to clarify some decisions.
- Umpire uses both hands to make a rectangular (TV screen) shape in front of their body.

PENALTY RUNS
Given for things like time-wasting and damaging the pitch.
- Umpire crosses one arm on to opposite shoulder.

CANCEL CALL
When umpire wishes to amend their decision and cancel the previous signal.
- Umpire touches both hands onto opposite shoulders in cross-over motion.

Modern thinking in sports coaching now recognises that there are four key performance factors that underpin the development of a player. These are technical, tactical, physical and mental. In the past much coaching was of a highly technical nature, with tactical ability being learned through experience. The physical and mental aspects of the game were often completely ignored. However, the approach to coaching the game has changed significantly in the past few years, and throughout this manual all four performance areas will be considered. This is done on the basis that skills can be developed in each of these areas, and that this will help in the all-round development of the player.

THE FOUR CORNERSTONES OF

TECHNICAL

Developing a proper technique has for many years been the 'holy grail' of cricketers. The MCC Coaching Manual was seen as the bible for 'correct' technique, with its explanations and illustrations of the correct technical models for coaches to use and players to copy. Other manuals have also been written over the years by individual authors, and they explain in great technical detail how the game should be played. From these, it would appear on balance that a core group of technical principles have remained constant, even though each generation has brought a slightly different flavour to how things should be done. Such variations generally reflect the prevailing trends at the time of writing.

The amount of science and research applied to cricket has increased significantly over the past few years, and the scientific study of movement and biomechanics now underpins the technical principles being applied to the modern game. As they have always done, these common principles would appear to give players the best chance of success when executing the skills of the game.

The most significant shift in modern coaching techniques would appear to be the recognition that players are all different and that there is no single correct technical model. This does not, however, mean that we should throw traditional views of the technical model out of the window, but rather that we should apply the technical principles with discretion to help enhance a player's natural abilities.

TACTICAL

The general definition of a tactic is a concept or course of action designed to achieve a specific outcome. It is generally accepted that cricket is by nature a very tactical game. Teams and individuals use many tactics during a match to try and achieve successful outcomes that will help them win the game.

As was pointed out above, tactical awareness and the use of tactics was historically allowed to develop along with a player's experience. This is still the case today, but it is now generally accepted that developing tactical awareness and the ability to apply tactics successfully are abilities that can be taught and developed.

Modern coaching techniques champion the use of modified games, which allow the 'game to be the teacher'. Other techniques utilised to help players develop tactical play include the use of simulated match situations, which enable them to understand tactical play in a match context, and also the use of classroom-style scenarios which allow them to discuss potential options that will help achieve success. Many of these approaches have been taken by coaches throughout the history of the game and are therefore not new, but such performance-enhancing methods have recently become more recognised and are now integrated into the training and development of young players.

PERFORMANCE

PHYSICAL

MENTAL

In the area of physical development cricket has been very limited by tradition, having in the past actively promoted itself as a technical, skill-based game which required endurance and stamina and little else. This made proper physical preparation seem somehow unnecessary. The truth, however, is that cricket requires speed, power and agility to effectively utilise the many diverse skills required to play the game. Fortunately times are changing, and cricket at higher levels has now embraced the need for proper physical preparation.

It is important, nevertheless, that cricket should remain a sport for all shapes and sizes at recreational level, as this has always been one of the game's attractions. But the hard fact that speed and power are essential to execute many of the skills of the game well should not be lost sight of. Nor that agility is a vital ingredient for success, particularly in the field. There is no doubt that limited-overs cricket has played a part in the need for better fitness levels, as fielding and quick runs have become more important, and the increased popularity of Twenty 20 cricket will only accelerate this need.

It is important to understand that physical preparation will continue to be an important performance factor.

It has long been accepted that a strong mind is a key performance factor in cricket. The best players throughout history have all been described as mentally tough, whether batters or bowlers. What has been less clear, however, has been how players can set about developing mental skills that would help improve their performance. Cricketing tradition has again put developing mental strength down to experience instead of accepting that there are methods that coaches can teach and that players can adopt to improve the way they think on the field.

As a result of changes to coaching education programmes, cricket coaches are now integrating the development of mental skills into training sessions. Introducing things such as decision-making drills into training programmes is becoming commonplace at all levels of the game and has obvious benefits for all players, and especially the batters. Other methods such as introducing routines to aid concentration, positive self-talk to aid confidence and goal-setting to benefit mental attitudes and approach to training, are all being used increasingly to help improve performance.

In addition to the four key performance areas described here, 'performance lifestyle' is often referred to as a fifth performance factor. This, however, tends to relate to the higher levels of the game and preparing for life as a professional athlete. It should be recognised, nevertheless, that living a healthy lifestyle will always benefit performance, irrespective of the level of the player.

PHYSICAL PREPARATION

Andrew Flintoff boxes with trainer Reg Dickason during a fitness session

As discussed earlier, cricket coaching has for many years focused the majority of its energy on developing the technical and tactical skills required to help batters to be successful. While it was recognised that physical fitness would help aid performance, it was not seen as a top priority and the type of fitness promoted was very general in nature.

In order to identify the specific physical skills that will best aid a player's performance, it is important first to consider exactly what the player does. Cricket consists of various key physical components, and these include: endurance, to help successfully execute their technique for longer; speed, which helps in both skill execution and in running between the wickets; strength and power, which helps them to hit the ball harder and further and

to move more quickly; and agility, which promotes efficiency of movement, stretch and reach in order to improve technical execution.

It is beneficial for any cricketer to have a training programme that will help develop these physical skills and in turn help them become more effective. However, it is important that any cricket-specific programme is properly understood and followed within the context of an overall training programme. This may also involve training for other sports. Players should always consult their coach or seek professional advice to ensure that training programmes are appropriate to age, fitness and time of year. It is also possible and highly beneficial for coaches to integrate physical training into cricket-specific training programmes. This tends to make the

ENGLAND
CRICKET

training more game-specific. Other elements of training, however, are better done outside a cricket environment, and listed below are some of the general types of training that help develop physical skills for cricketers:

ENDURANCE TRAINING
Aerobic training
This may be a combination of the following but recognises running as the most important and specific to cricket.
- Distance running for 25–35 minutes.
- Cycling for 30–40 minutes.
- Interval training (multiple sets of running hard for four minutes, walking for four minutes, etc).
- Gymnasium CV machines (rowing machine, stepper, cross trainer, etc).

SPEED TRAINING
Anaerobic training
This should include speed endurance training.
- Enhancement of running technique (limbs moving in direction of travel, fast foot ladders, etc).
- Resistance sprint training (using bands with partner, parachutes, etc).
- Multiple sprint runs (10 x 20–30m, etc).

STRENGTH AND POWER
Repetitive overloading of muscles
Cricketers should generally look to be strong throughout the length of their body.
- Core strength training (static holds, Swiss balls, etc).
- Body weight training (push-ups, chin-ups, etc).
- Weight training (bench press, free weights, gym machines, etc).

(Weight training is generally discouraged for young children. Any training can usually be done using own body weight.)

AGILITY TRAINING
Balance and co-ordination
Improving the player's ability to change direction efficiently.
- Dynamic balance training (using quick changes of direction, speed agility ladders etc).
- Pilates, yoga and stretching exercises.

Kevin Pietersen doing shuttle runs during a training session

MENTAL PREPARATION

Australia's Matthew Hayden carries out a pre-match visualisation routine

The training and development of mental skills is arguably the most neglected area of performance in cricket. For years it was assumed that a player was either mentally strong or not, and no effort was ever made to try and train or develop their use of mental skills to improve performance. This was despite the fact that sports psychologists had been operating for decades in many other sports to great success.

More recently it has been recognised that the training of mental skills is fundamental in helping toimprove performance in what is the most mentally challenging of sports. There is a simple rule-of-thumb equation used in sports psychology which states:

Performance = Ability minus Distractions

The most important of the mental skills required to perform well in cricket – and indeed in any sport – are those that enable the player to minimise the distracting negative thoughts, doubts and general interferences that hinder performance. It has long been recognised that the most 'mentally tough' players display certain mental attributes which help them to maintain high performance levels irrespective of the situation. The four main attributes, which are known as 'the four Cs', are:

- Confidence
- Concentration
- Control
- Consistency

ENGLAND CRICKET

As stated before, it is now accepted by players and coaches alike that it is possible to train and develop these mental skills, and although sports psychologists play an important part in developing such skills, particularly at the top levels of the game, it does not require a trained sports psychologist to teach what are, in essence, a set of commonsense principles.

There are several very basic techniques that coaches and players can use to help develop mentally strong cricketers, as follows.

PERFORMANCE PROFILING/ GOAL-SETTING

Identifying where a player's performance-related strengths and weaknesses lie. This can be done by the player on their own or jointly with their coach. It is usually done using a simple 1–10 scale, and allows goals to be set and a programme of training to be developed that will help improve the player's performance in each of the identified areas. Although originally designed for use in the development of mental skills, this is an ideal tool for use in the technical areas of batting, bowling and fielding and, indeed, helps to encourage self-awareness and confidence and brings a consistent approach to training and performance.

POSITIVE THINKING

Sometimes popularly known as 'positive mental attitude', this can help players develop and maintain consistent performances while coping with the inevitable mental stresses involved in competition. It is important that players believe that they have the ability to overcome the challenges which lie before them. Positive self-talk is one such technique that can help players cope with pressure. This involves the player having a small list of positive statements about themselves in their mind which they can draw on in times of stress. These statements can also be repeated daily to help build confidence. These tend to be simple statements which the player can relate to personally such as, 'I am playing well in training' or 'I am strong enough to succeed' or 'my coach believes in me'. Another well-tried technique is to build a list of 'achievement reminders', such as 'I got a hundred against this team last year' or 'Averages prove I am the best player here'.

VISUALISATION/IMAGERY

Sometimes known as 'going to the movies', using mental imagery has been shown to be very effective in helping players improve performance. It simply involves playing over in the mind an image of the skills that are about to be performed being successfully accomplished. Successful use of imagery can also go beyond seeing things played over in the mind; imagining how the skill *feels* when performed successfully can also help to increase the chances of success. In essence visualisation is the reproduction in the mind of all the information the senses need to successfully execute a skill. The use of mental imagery should also be used regularly to support training and to help develop confidence in the successful application of a player's cricket skills.

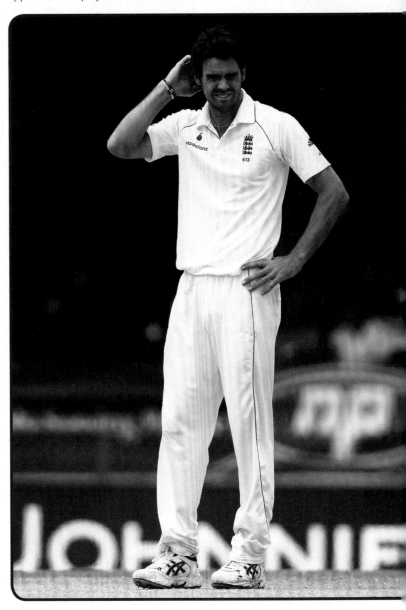

James Anderson contemplates events during a bowling spell against the West Indies

2
BATTING

INTRODUCTION TO BATTING

The essence of cricket is the age-old contest between bat and ball. The batters' job is to score as many runs as possible and the bowlers' job is to get them out. In the following section we will deal with batting and the business of scoring runs.

Throughout the history of cricket it is the great batsmen who have always been most fondly remembered. Names like W.G. Grace, Donald Bradman, Viv Richards, Brian Lara and Sachin Tendulkar all trip off the tongue of the cricket fan as the greatest batsmen of their time and true legends of the game.

Batting is seen by many as the most important discipline in cricket, and indeed most spectators who attend a cricket match do so to see the artistry and power of the best batters. The bowlers may, however, have something to say about this assertion, and the truth is that neither is more important than the other. Nowadays, though, you can often hear both players and coaches say "it's a batters' game", and this has become increasingly the case since the advent of limited overs' matches. This form of the game has put a premium on scoring runs quickly and made the taking of wickets less important. In both 50-over and 20-over matches playing conditions have been introduced which provide greater opportunities for batters to score runs quickly.

The rise of Twenty 20 cricket has further accelerated the need for batters to be able to score quick runs. As a result batters now adopt a far more positive outlook in terms of run-scoring. This more positive approach has highlighted the risk and reward nature of cricket and is reflected in the type of cricket that predominates today. Matches now tend to be more entertaining than in the past, with batters taking greater risks to try and score runs. It should also be remembered that this increased risk provides greater opportunities for bowlers as well, and the balanced nature of this contest is a fundamental part of cricket's great attraction. The prevalence of attacking play is also now having an impact on the longer forms of the game, where scoring rates are steadily increasing to reflect the more attacking approach adopted by modern batters.

Due to the nature of cricket and the fact that the ball is being bowled by an opponent, batting is deemed to be an 'open' skill. This means the successful execution of any shot is dependent on the batter deciding where, when and how the ball will arrive and deciding what shot to play within the tactical context of the match. The successful technical execution of the shot then further depends on the physical and mental ability of the batter to apply the skill. In addition to this a further decision on whether or not to run has to be made in conjunction with the other batter. As one can see, therefore, the successful outcome for a batter in any one ball is dependent on many factors and is a highly complex process. Add to this the need for a batter to do this repeatedly over a long period of time to be successful, and one can see why batting is such a great challenge.

Hopefully the previous passage has shown that successful batting is about much more than being technically proficient, and that all four key performance factors are involved. This is reinforced by the fact that:

- Technique is important, and the science that underpins the correct technical model undoubtedly gives a batter the best chance of success.
- It is also clear that this success is dependent on good decision-making and cognitive (mental) ability.
- The tactics being applied and the context of the game will also impact on the decision-making process, proving that tactical awareness is also a key factor in being successful.
- In addition to all these things, physical abilities such as speed, agility and aerobic endurance are likely to play a significant role in whether a batter is able to successfully execute the skills required.

In summary, the two most significant modern advances in the development of batting are:

- The more positive approach taken by batters to run-scoring. This requires an aggressive mindset and a commitment to develop an effective repertoire of attacking scoring options.
- A more 'holistic' approach to the development of batting skills, considering not only technical skill development but also recognising the need to develop tactical, physical and mental performance.

Surrey openers walk out to the wicket

Bangladesh player Rajin Saleh bats in the nets during a practice session

ENGLAND CRICKET

BATTERS' EQUIPMENT

Given the hard nature of a cricket ball, it is important that a batter has the appropriate bat to score runs with and the correct safety equipment to protect vulnerable parts of the body. Obvious equipment such as helmets are crucial to protect players from serious injury (all players under 18 in the UK must wear a helmet in an organised practice or match). Other pieces of safety equipment are less visible but no less important. The following is a guide to the most important items that a batter may need or choose to wear.

BAT
1 Many different types of bat are available, including bat 'shapes' – made out of plastic or other materials – suitable for use in modified games where softer balls are used. When a cricket ball is used, however, a willow bat is required. Willow bats come in a variety of sizes and weights.

The size of the bat is usually related to the batter's height. A good rule of thumb for the best bat size is that the top of the handle should reach to the top of the thigh when both player and bat are in an upright position.

The appropriate weight is more subjective, with adult bats generally weighing between 2lb and 3lb. Children's bats should be lighter than those used by adults, and too light rather than too heavy is usually a good rule of thumb. Lighter bats tend to help develop a more rounded technique that allows batters to play effective cross and straight shots. Eager but thrifty parents should not be drawn into the trap of buying a big bat for their child to grow into, as a heavy and unwieldy bat can quite often be detrimental to the development of a sound technique.

PADS
2 Pads should always be worn on both legs when a hard ball is in use. They are designed to protect the ankles, shins, knees and lower thighs. Again parents should beware of pads that are too big, as they can interfere with running and even shot-making. Pads that are too small and do not cover above the knee are also ineffective and dangerous.

Modern pads tend to be held in place by at least two or three Velcro straps and are available in right- and left-handed versions. Pads also come in various levels of protective quality, which is normally reflected in the price. Cricketers playing in higher-level matches, where the ball is travelling faster, are advised to use pads of the best quality.

GLOVES
3 Like pads, gloves should be worn at all times when playing or practising with a hard ball. A wide variety of gloves are available and in a range of protective qualities. Also be aware that gloves are available in both left- and right-handed versions to provide extra protection for the thumb of the bottom hand.

HELMET
4 As stated above, the ECB (England and Wales Cricket Board), supported by the governing bodies of the other home nations within the UK, have issued safety guidance on the compulsory wearing of helmets by all players under the age of 18. This applies to all young batters in both adult and junior cricket played with a hard ball. The helmets worn should have a grille to protect the face and be made by a recognised manufacturer of cricket helmets. It is also crucial that each helmet should be of the correct size to fit the wearer.

ABDOMINAL PROTECTOR (BOX)
5 Male cricketers should always wear an abdominal guard, or 'box' as it is more commonly known, to protect their genitals and lower abdomen.

THIGH GUARDS
6 Thigh guards are used to protect the soft tissue on the upper leg and thigh. Outer thigh guards (placed on the outside of the upper leg that faces the bowler) have traditionally been worn in all forms of the game played with a hard ball. Inner thigh guards, which protect the inside thigh on the back leg, were originally used in the professional game where the bowling was faster, but are now commonly used in all forms of the game.

ARM AND CHEST GUARDS
7 These are more normally used at the higher levels of the game where the bowlers are faster and the ball regularly bounces to chest height and above. As with inner thigh guards, however, they are becoming more common in all forms of the game to reduce the risk of injury.

BATTERS' SET-UP

TAKING GUARD

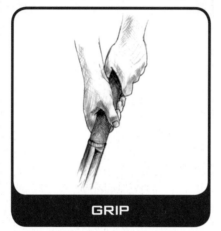

GRIP

BACKSWING (AND STEP)

When a batter first arrives at the crease to begin their innings they will ask the umpire for a 'guard', so called because it relates to their ability to guard the stumps. This is done as shown above. The three most commonly requested guards are:

■ Leg stump (this guard is also sometimes requested by simply asking for 'one').
■ Middle and Leg (which is a line midway between middle and leg stumps; also known as 'two').
■ Middle stump (also known as 'centre').

The umpire then verbally guides the bat to the requested guard. The batter marks the ground at that guard so that they can place their bat, and in turn their head and body, in a consistent position in relation to their stumps. The best position is generally regarded to be with the head above middle stump, but this is a matter of personal preference.

This is extremely important as it is the basis from which the hands work together to control the movement of the bat.

STANCE

This position should be relaxed, comfortable and balanced, allowing good vision to track the ball and a clear path for the bat to swing back and then forward to make contact. Many batters also use a rhythmic 'bat tap' while in the stance position.

Once the batter has established a relaxed and comfortable stance that allows the ball to be tracked, it is important that the body moves smoothly – using sound mechanics – into a balanced position. This allows the player to successfully execute the chosen shot. Some players use a pre-delivery or 'trigger' movement to get their 'engine running' and initiate their movement sequence, while some choose to stand still. It is up to the individual to find out what works best for them. But what is clear is that once the shot selection has been made, any foot movement and backswing should be made in unison to provide the most efficient, balanced movement and give best chance of success.

ENGLAND CRICKET

Paul Collingwood demonstrates a good set-up position as he prepares to step towards the ball while commencing his backswing

KEY POINTS

GRIP

- Right hand below left for a right-handed batter and left hand below right for a left-hander
- Fingers and thumbs wrapped around the handle
- Ideally two aligned 'Vs' should be formed by the thumb and index finger of each hand centred between the outside edge and back of the bat
- Hands close together and working together, ideally somewhere near or just above the middle of the handle

STANCE

- Feet should be parallel and a comfortable distance apart to form a good base
- Weight should be distributed evenly with knees slightly flexed to allow for quick movement and weight transfer either backward or forward
- Body should be in a relaxed side-on position
- Eyes level and directly over base

BACKSWING (AND STEP)

- Front shoulder rolls down as bat swings back
- Bat handle and hands stay close to body underneath shoulders
- Co-ordinated movement and comfortable stride backward or forward
- Head should move smoothly towards the line of the ball

PRE-DELIVERY MOVEMENT

When batters first learn to play the game they are generally encouraged to remain quite still in their stance until commencing the backswing and step as the ball is delivered. As players grow older the ball is bowled at faster speeds and batters have less time to react and decide which shot to play. As a result many players choose to use a pre-delivery or 'trigger' movement just prior to the ball being delivered. This helps initiate their body movement and place them in a better state of readiness to play the ball. There are two principal types of movement:

- **Forward press** – When the batter makes a small forward movement with the front foot towards the line of the ball, moving their weight into a slightly forward position while retaining their balance.

- **Back and across** – When the batter makes a movement back and across, generally towards the middle and off stumps, moving their weight into a slight backward position while retaining their balance.

It is a matter of individual preference for a batter whether or not to use a trigger and, if so, which type they prefer. There are two key elements required for a pre-delivery movement to be effective: firstly, consistent timing and distance of the movement; secondly, retaining a balanced position that still allows comfortable forward and backward movement. There is, however, a danger that these movements, when poorly executed, can over-complicate movement patterns and hinder rather than benefit the batter. Young players are encouraged to work closely with their coach when considering the development of a pre-delivery movement.

OBSERVATION, DECISION-MAKING AND SHOT SELECTION

Good observation, decision-making and shot selections are crucial if a batter is to be consistently successful. Firstly, the batter must observe both the bowler and ball closely to pick up some clues as to where and how the ball is liable to arrive. This information is picked up by reading a series of cues from both the bowler and the early flight-path of the ball. These cues are picked up by observing the bowler in their run-up and being aware of certain key things such as their position on the crease, front-arm movement, bowling-arm speed and angle, etc.

The primary focus just prior to and after release, however, should always be the position of the bowler's hand and the seam of the ball. These crucial cues, along with the early flight of the ball, give the batter critical information that will allow them to predict how and where the ball is likely to arrive and to decide exactly what course of action to take. This information informs a series of decisions, which include: to play or not to play, to play forward or back, and to attack or defend. The batter must then select an appropriate stroke from their repertoire. The majority of dismissals in cricket matches at all levels can be put down partly to poor shot selection, so the importance of this skill should not be underestimated.

The batter has around a dozen strokes to choose from, give or take a few variations on themes. Decisions on which stroke to play will normally be related to the observation and prediction of line and length as stated above. It is generally accepted in cricketing terminology that there are three main lines and five main lengths of delivery which tend to impact on the range of shots that a batter may choose to play.

ORTHODOX AND UNORTHODOX STROKES

The different types of strokes played by a batter tend to vary depending on where the ball pitches. The strokes that are traditionally regarded as the most effective are shown on the page opposite in relation to the general area where the ball pitches. It should be noted that these pitching zones are shown as a guide only. They derive from what has been historically regarded as giving the batter the best chance of success.

Most of the top players generally conform to an orthodox technique but increasingly in the modern game are becoming more open-minded in their approach to scoring runs. Kevin Pietersen would be an obvious example of a batter who does not always conform to the generally accepted technical model for success. He is, however, highly effective and although he may be considered to be unorthodox, he has a fundamental technique that is extremely sound and highly orthodox.

It is important to remember that each individual batter is unique and should develop the technique that gives them their own best chance of success, irrespective of what other manuals may say. Individual flair is part of the beauty of cricket and should always be encouraged. In the end a successful outcome for the batter (ie, scoring runs) is what is important. One-day and Twenty 20 cricket have increased the number of innovative and creative shots used by batters, and one should never be scared to experiment with the unorthodox in practice, and, if it works, to use it in a game. The unorthodox, however, tends to flourish from a sound technical base.

THE DIFFERENT LINES AND LENGTHS

THE THREE MAIN LINES

- Wide of off stump
- Straight (from just wide of off stump to middle stump)
- Leg stump and outside

THE FIVE MAIN LENGTHS

- Bouncer or long hop (depending on pace)
- Short/back of a length
- Good length
- Full length/half volley
- Full toss/beamer (depending on height)

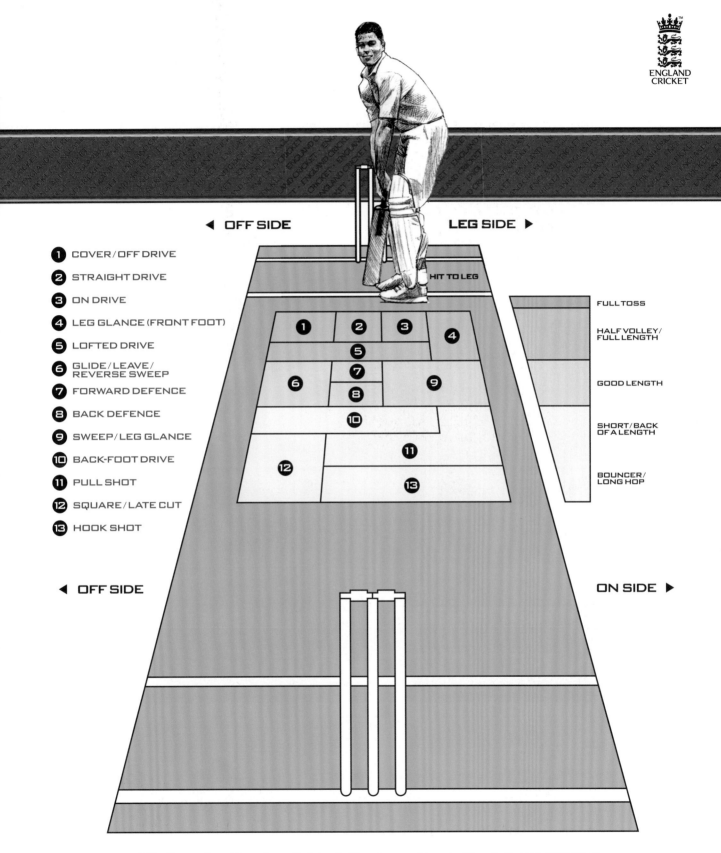

◀ OFF SIDE   LEG SIDE ▶

HIT TO LEG

① COVER/OFF DRIVE

② STRAIGHT DRIVE

③ ON DRIVE

④ LEG GLANCE (FRONT FOOT)

⑤ LOFTED DRIVE

⑥ GLIDE/LEAVE/ REVERSE SWEEP

⑦ FORWARD DEFENCE

⑧ BACK DEFENCE

⑨ SWEEP/LEG GLANCE

⑩ BACK-FOOT DRIVE

⑪ PULL SHOT

⑫ SQUARE/LATE CUT

⑬ HOOK SHOT

FULL TOSS

HALF VOLLEY/ FULL LENGTH

GOOD LENGTH

SHORT/BACK OF A LENGTH

BOUNCER/ LONG HOP

◀ OFF SIDE   ON SIDE ▶

This diagram is not to scale and is intended to act as a guide only. The actual measurements of where these lines and lengths start and finish are only in the batter's mind and are dependent on many other variables, such as pace, bounce, lateral movement, type of surface and so on

STRAIGHT-BAT SHOTS

FRONT-FOOT DRIVE

STRAIGHT DRIVE PITCHING ZONE

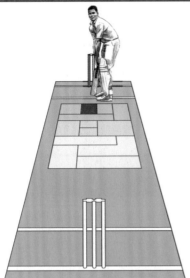

STRAIGHT DRIVE HITTING ZONE

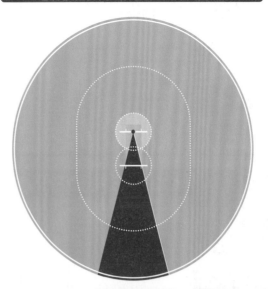

Andrew Flintoff hits a straight drive while playing against South Africa

The front-foot drive is probably the most graceful shot in cricket when played well. It is an attacking stroke played with the intention of beating the field and scoring runs. It is normally played to a ball of full length. The front-foot drive has several variations, which usually depend on where the ball pitches and as a result affect where the ball is normally hit to. The typical scoring areas for a front-foot drive are between cover point on the off side and mid-on on the leg side.

STRAIGHT DRIVE

This is normally played back past the bowler straight down the ground to a half volley or full-pitch ball on or around an off or middle stump line. The area behind the bowler is often unprotected and the reward for this stroke can often be four runs. The straight drive, as with all shots, is best played from a strong set-up position with a good grip and a relaxed and balanced stance.

KEY POINTS

- Relaxed and balanced stance
- Eyes level and watching the ball
- Head, shoulders and front foot move towards the line of the ball
- Front shoulder dips to counterbalance backswing
- Head stays steady with eyes level and fixed on the ball
- Front foot stabilises and knee bends
- Weight transfers forward to create a stable base
- Shoulders initiate downswing and rotate downwards vertically
- Bat accelerates vertically to the point of contact
- Contact made underneath the eyes
- Bat and hands accelerate through the contact area and out after the ball
- Balance maintained throughout

OFF DRIVE

This stroke is normally hit on the off side of the wicket, just wide of the mid-off fielding position to a full-length ball on or just outside the off stump. The shot is played with a very similar technique to the straight drive.

Michael Vaughan

COVER DRIVE

This stroke is also hit to the offside of the ground, but slightly wider or squarer of the wicket than the off drive. The shot is intended to pierce the field in the gap between cover and extra cover. It is normally played to a full-length or fuller good-length ball pitching outside the off stump. Again the technique is very similar to the other drives, but the movement of the head, shoulders and foot across to the line of the ball is crucial. Sometimes the shot is actually more of an off drive with the face opened to alter the path of the ball through the field.

Andrew Strauss

ON DRIVE

This is the only drive to the leg side of the wicket, and is hit with the intention of beating the mid-on fielder. The stroke is normally played to a full-length ball on or around a leg-stump line. Again the principles remain the same as the other drives with the exception of a shortened stride towards the ball which makes it easier to remain balanced through the shot.

Kevin Pietersen

LOFTED DRIVE

This is played when the batter deliberately wants to hit the ball in the air. The objective is either to beat the infield or to hit a six. This is normally played to a full-length or fuller good-length ball and can be applied to a ball on any driveable line, from wide of off stump all the way to leg stump. The basic principles, as always with the drives, are very similar, but the ball does tend to be struck slightly earlier than with the other drives, and the batter's weight usually remains slightly back in comparison.

Claire Taylor

MOVING OUT TO DRIVE

This tactical manoeuvre is used principally against spin but occasionally against medium-pace bowling. It involves the batter advancing down the pitch to 'change the length' and create more scoring opportunities. This stroke tends to be played to a ball that would have been deemed a good-length ball and may well have been defended had the batter not advanced down the wicket. This stroke is often premeditated and involves a double step towards the ball. It is very important that the batter remains in a low, balanced position throughout the movement to retain balance and create a stable base to hit through.

Ed Joyce

PITCHING ZONE

HITTING ZONE

PITCHING ZONE

HITTING ZONE

PITCHING ZONE

HITTING ZONE

PITCHING ZONE

HITTING ZONE

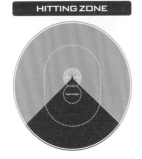

PITCHING ZONE

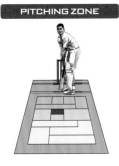

HITTING ZONE

STRAIGHT-BAT SHOTS

FORWARD DEFENSIVE

FORWARD DEFENSIVE PITCHING ZONE

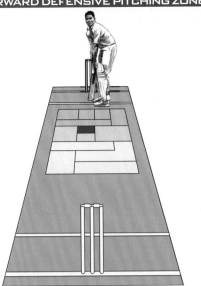

KEY POINTS

- Relaxed and balanced stance
- Eyes level and watching the ball
- Head, shoulders and front foot move towards the line of the ball
- Front shoulder dips to counterbalance backswing
- Head stays steady with eyes level and fixed on the ball
- Comfortable stride forward
- Front foot stabilises and knee bends
- Weight transfers forward to create a stable base
- Shoulders initiate downswing and rotate downwards vertically
- Bat first accelerates then decelerates vertically to the point of contact
- Contact made underneath the eyes
- Full face of the bat presented to the ball
- Bottom-hand grip relaxed to create 'soft hands'
- Balance maintained throughout
- Awareness of run-scoring opportunities

Michael Brown of Hampshire defends during a county championship match

The forward defensive is a crucial part of any batter's armoury. It is designed to stop the ball and is normally played with a dead bat directed downwards to prevent the batter from being caught. It is normally played to a good-length ball that would otherwise have hit or passed close to the stumps. Traditionally this shot was not intended to be a run-scoring option, but in the modern game a well-placed forward defensive can often be a great opportunity to 'steal' a quick run.

The forward defensive used to be the first stroke taught to any young batter when the game traditionally adopted a 'defend first and attack if you can' approach to batting. The front-foot drive, which is closely related to the forward defensive due to the many similarities in technique, was always seen as a second, more 'high-risk' option. Fortunately, times have changed and the modern cricket mindset tends to have more of an 'attack first and defend if you can't' approach. This has not only made the game more entertaining but has

made learning it more fun as well. Nowadays the front-foot drive is often the first stroke taught, with the forward defensive taught second as a fall-back. The reality is that these shots, once learned, should be practised together within a well-planned decision-training session which gives the option to attack and defend balls of varying length pitching on the appropriate line.

As already stated, many of the basic principles for the forward defensive are similar to those of the straight or front-foot drives. This includes the essential strong set-up position.

STRAIGHT-BAT SHOTS

BACK-FOOT DRIVE

BACK-FOOT DRIVE PITCHING ZONE

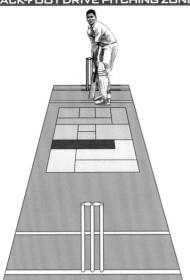

BACK-FOOT DRIVE HITTING ZONE

ENGLAND CRICKET

Michael Vaughan hits a back-foot drive through the covers

The back-foot drive is the principal straight-bat attacking option for back-foot play. It tends to be seen more at higher levels of the game where the ball is being delivered at greater speeds and the surfaces are more hard and true. This should not, however, prevent a young player from learning and practising how to play this shot effectively. This can be done easily using a tennis ball on a hard surface to replicate more pace and bounce – this can sometimes be difficult to achieve with a cricket ball on a softer grass or non-turf pitch.

The objective of the back-foot drive is to pierce the field and score runs. The stroke is normally played to a short-of-a-length delivery, bouncing to around stump height. Depending on its line, the ball tends to be hit in an arc from the cover point fielding position around to mid-on.

KEY POINTS

- Relaxed and balanced stance
- Eyes level and watching the ball
- Head, shoulders and back foot move back and towards the line of the ball
- Front shoulder dips to counterbalance backswing
- Head stays steady with eyes level and fixed on the ball
- Back foot stabilises, ideally as parallel to the crease as possible
- Weight transfers backwards to create a stable base
- Head should remain forward of back leg to maintain balanced position
- Shoulders initiate downswing and rotate downwards vertically
- Bat accelerates vertically to the point of contact
- Front leg is withdrawn backwards to balance movement of bat towards ball
- Contact made underneath the eyes
- Bat and hands accelerate through the contact area and out after the ball
- Balance maintained throughout

STRAIGHT-BAT SHOTS

BACK DEFENSIVE

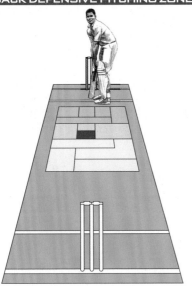

ENGLAND CRICKET

KEY POINTS

- Relaxed and balanced stance
- Eyes level and watching the ball
- Head, shoulders and back foot move back and towards the line of the ball
- Front shoulder dips to counterbalance backswing
- Head stays steady with eyes level and fixed on the ball
- Back foot stabilises, ideally as parallel as possible to the crease
- Weight transfers backwards to create a stable base
- Head should remain forward of back leg to maintain balanced position
- Shoulders initiate downswing and rotate downwards vertically
- Bat accelerates then decelerates vertically to the point of contact
- Front leg is withdrawn backwards to balance movement of bat towards ball
- Contact made underneath the eyes
- Full face of the bat presented to the ball
- Bottom-hand grip relaxed to create 'soft hands'
- Balance maintained throughout
- Awareness of run-scoring opportunities

The back defensive, like the forward defensive, is very closely related to its attacking sister stroke. There are many similarities between the back-foot drive and defensive shot. This stroke is designed to stop the ball and should normally be played with a dead bat and directed downwards to prevent the batter being caught. It is usually played to a ball of a good length (or slightly shorter) that would otherwise have hit the stumps or passed over or close to them. Like the forward defensive, this stroke was not originally intended to be a run-scoring option, but a well-placed back defence can result in a quick single if both batters are 'on the ball'.

The back defensive also used to be taught before its attacking sister stroke, but, as with the front-foot shots, the drive now tends to be taught first. As before, the reality is that these back-foot shots are so similar that once learned they should be developed together. This can be done in well-structured decision-training sessions that allow batters to develop their ability to play both these strokes successfully to the appropriate ball.

Kevin Pietersen gets off the ground to defend a sharply rising delivery

LEG GLANCE

Sarah Taylor

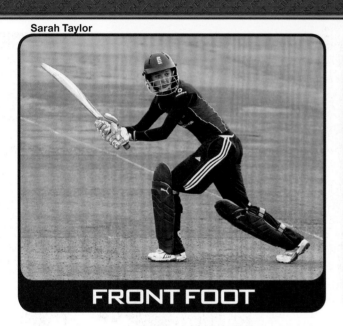

FRONT FOOT

Alastair Cook

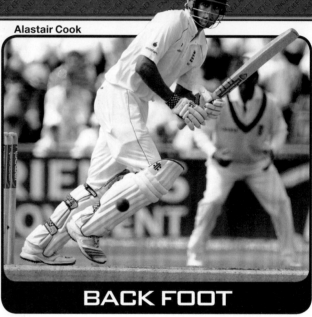

BACK FOOT

An attacking shot, normally played against medium or quicker paced bowlers, which uses the pace of the ball to deflect it past the wicketkeeper towards the boundary behind square on the leg side of the wicket. This stroke is normally played to a full-length delivery on or outside the leg stump. The principles of the stroke are very similar to the other front-foot straight-bat shots, with the differing key points of:

- Ensure the line of the ball is leg side and move front leg towards the line of the ball.
- Turn wrists as contact is made to guide the ball behind square.

This is an attacking shot which can be played against bowling of any pace but is now used frequently against spin bowling. This stroke also uses the pace of the ball to deflect it behind square on the leg side, and against spin can sometimes go just in front of square on the leg side. It is normally played to a good-length or short-of-a-length delivery on or outside the leg stump. The principles of this shot are very similar to the other back-foot straight-bat shots, with the differing key points of:

- Ensure the line of the ball is leg side and withdraw the front leg in line with the ball.
- Turn the wrists as contact is made to guide the ball on to the leg side.

PITCHING ZONE	HITTING ZONE

PITCHING ZONE	HITTING ZONE

OFF-SIDE GLIDE

Ian Bell

BACK FOOT

This attacking shot is generally played against the medium or quicker paced bowlers and uses the pace of the ball to run it down towards the boundary at third man (the shot is also known, somewhat unsurprisingly, as the 'run down to third man'). It has become increasingly popular since the advent of limited-overs cricket and is normally played to a short-of-a-length ball outside the off stump. This delivery may well be left by the batter in longer forms of the game, but limited-overs cricket demands that runs are scored more frequently and leaving the ball is rarely an option. The basic principles of the stroke are similar to those of the back-foot defensive, with the following different key points:

- At the point of contact the face of the bat should be opened slightly to guide the ball behind square on the off side.
- The stroke should be played with 'soft hands' and the ball should be allowed to hit the face of the bat.

PITCHING ZONE

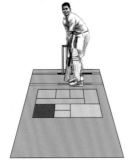

HITTING ZONE

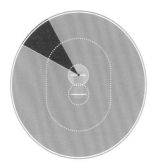

CROSS-BAT SHOTS

PULL SHOT

PULL SHOT PITCHING ZONE

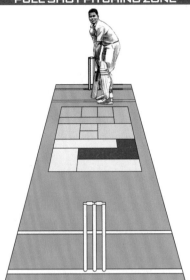

PULL SHOT HITTING ZONE

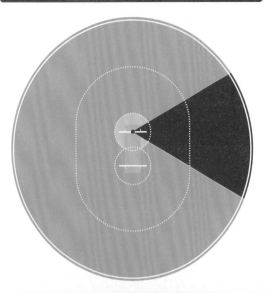

ENGLAND
CRICKET

Paul Collingwood
pulls a ball past
the South African
short leg fielder

When played well the pull and hook shots can be the most dynamic and powerful shots in cricket. The pull shot is an attacking back-foot shot played with a cross bat and is intended to be hit to the leg-side boundary. The pull is played to a short delivery which is usually passing over the stumps or outside the leg stump. The technique used when playing the pull shot can vary depending on the pace of the ball. The illustrations below show the withdrawal and planting of the front leg into a solid base position prior to contact. This is usually only possible against the slower bowlers. Against quicker bowling the withdrawal of the front leg normally takes place after contact, as shown in the picture of Paul Collingwood.

The fundamental principles of the cross-bat shots are similar in nature to the straight-bat shots until the top of the backswing. From there the path of the bat travels horizontally for cross-bat shots, as opposed to the vertical path followed in straight-bat shots.

KEY POINTS

- Relaxed and balanced stance
- Eyes level and watching the ball
- Head, shoulders and back foot move back and across to the off side
- Front leg moves back and across to the leg side to create a stable base
- Head stays steady with eyes level and fixed on the ball
- Head should remain forward of back leg to maintain balanced position
- At the top of the backswing the weight transfers back on to the front leg
- Shoulders rotate horizontally, accelerating the bat towards contact
- Contact made below the eyes and in front of the body
- Full face of the bat presented to the ball with hands extended
- Full follow-through after the ball
- Balance maintained throughout

CROSS-BAT SHOTS

SQUARE CUT

SQUARE CUT PITCHING ZONE

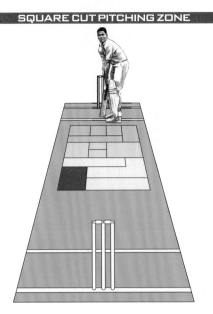

SQUARE CUT HITTING ZONE

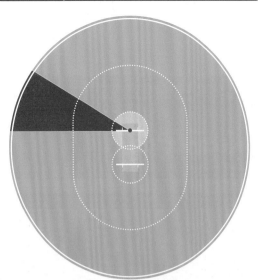

ENGLAND CRICKET

The cut shot, like the pull shot, is a powerful and dynamic cross-bat stroke played off the back foot. It is intended to pierce the field square of the wicket on the off side, and is played to a short delivery which bounces between thigh and chest height and is wide of off stump. Like the back-foot drive, the cut shot tends to be seen more at higher levels of the game where the ball is being delivered at greater speeds and the surfaces are hard and true. Once again, however, this should not prevent a young player from learning and practising how to play it effectively. This can be done easily using a soft ball or tennis ball on a hard surface to replicate more pace and bounce.

England keeper batsman Matt Prior plays a square cut

KEY POINTS

- Relaxed and balanced stance
- Eyes level and watching the ball
- Head, shoulders and back foot move back and across towards the line of the ball
- Head stays steady with eyes level and fixed on the ball
- Back foot stabilises as parallel as possible to the crease as weight transfers
- Shoulders rotate away from the ball
- Shoulders rotate, initiating the downswing towards the ball
- Contact is made as the ball comes level with the body
- Full follow-through after the ball
- Balance maintained throughout

HOOK SHOT

The hook shot is very similar in nature to the pull shot and is also an attacking cross-bat shot played off the back foot. It tends to be played to quicker short or very short pitched deliveries bouncing to chest height or above. The hook is a riskier shot than the pull, with the batter unable to exercise as much control due to the nature of the higher bounce of the ball. The reward, however, is that when good contact is made the ball can often fly for six.

The key points for the hook are almost identical to the pull shot against medium-pace bowlers, with the following differences:

- From the top of the backswing to the point of contact the weight remains on the back foot.
- Head remains forward and inside the line of the bouncing ball to maintain balance and safety.

PITCHING ZONE

HITTING ZONE

Andrew Strauss plays a hook shot for Middlesex, against Surrey

ENGLAND
CRICKET

**Paul Collingwood plays a
delicate late cut shot**

LATE CUT

This is almost identical to the square cut other than that the ball is played slightly later to guide it finer of the wicket behind square on the off side. The late cut tends to be a less powerful shot than the square cut, with the pace of the ball being used to guide it towards third man. The differing key points are:

- Contact is made with the ball slightly behind the body.
- Hands remain 'soft' so that the ball runs off the face of the bat.

PITCHING ZONE

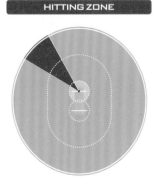

HITTING ZONE

CROSS-BAT SHOTS

SWEEP SHOT

Ian Bell gets in the ideal position to sweep

The sweep shot is an attacking front-foot cross-bat shot intended to score runs square or behind square of the wicket on the leg side. It is normally played to a good-length delivery anywhere on the leg side of a middle stump line. The sweep is normally utilised against spin, although more recently it has also been used against slower medium-paced bowlers as a tactical option against certain field settings.

In modern times the sweep has developed many different varieties including the reverse sweep, so called because the bat position is 'reversed' by changing the grip on the bat as the bowler is preparing to release the ball. This allows the batter to swing the bat in the opposite direction to the 'orthodox' sweep and hit the ball in the opposite direction square or behind square on the off side of the wicket. This shot is normally played to a good-length ball anywhere on the off side of the middle stump.

Other variations of the sweep have emerged as batters vary how hard they try to hit the ball when sweeping. In general the harder a batter hits the ball the squarer of the wicket it will travel. As a result the hard-hit 'slog' sweep has emerged where the batter hits the ball in front of square on the leg side. In

SWEEP SHOT PITCHING ZONE

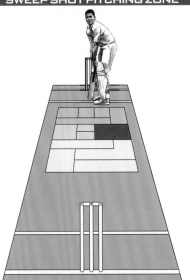

SWEEP SHOT HITTING ZONE

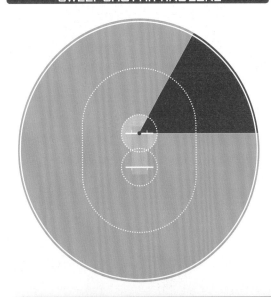

ENGLAND CRICKET

KEY POINTS

- Relaxed and balanced stance
- Eyes level and watching the ball
- Head, shoulders and front foot move towards the line of the ball
- Front shoulder dips to counterbalance backswing
- Head stays steady with eyes level and fixed on the ball
- Front foot stabilises and knee bends
- Back knee sinks close to or down on the ground to create a 'kneeling' position
- Weight transfers forward to create a stable base
- Shoulders rotate horizontally, accelerating the bat towards contact
- Contact made in line with the eyes and in front of the body
- Full face of the bat presented to the ball with hands extended
- Full follow-through after the ball
- Balance maintained throughout

contrast the softly hit 'lap' sweep involves the batter using the pace of the ball to direct it with 'soft hands' fine of the wicket. Batters will tend to exercise different tactical options depending on the field setting and the line of the ball.

Kevin Pietersen follows through with a sweep shot

CROSS-BAT SHOTS

REVERSE SWEEP SHOT

The basic principles for the reverse sweep are very similar to those of the more orthodox sweep, with the following different key points:

- Grip changes on the bat, rotating the handle by 180° and thus reversing the direction of the blade.
- As the front foot moves to create a solid base, the shoulders rotate horizontally by 180° with the opposite shoulder now facing the bowler, creating a reverse backswing.
- This allows the shoulders to rotate horizontally in the opposite direction to the orthodox sweep, accelerating the bat towards contact.

PITCHING ZONE

HITTING ZONE

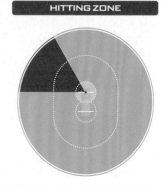

Ian Bell makes
contact with a
reverse sweep

ENGLAND
CRICKET

CREATIVE HITTING

Creative hitting is a loose term commonly used to describe shots that are not found anywhere in the traditional coaching manuals. These shots have only become commonplace in the game since the introduction of limited-overs cricket, and the rapid rise to prominence of Twenty 20 cricket has accelerated both the frequency and number of creative shots attempted.

The tactical rationale behind the use of creative or unorthodox shots is the ability of the batter to counter the tactics applied by the fielding side. Teams will try to bowl in certain areas and set fields to prevent run-scoring opportunities. Creative hitting therefore goes against the traditional conventions of where batters would normally hit the ball.

The West Indian legend of the 1970s and '80s, Vivian Richards, was the first great exponent of creative hitting. He was one of the first players to change his position at the crease when stepping back outside the leg stump to hit leg-side deliveries over the field on the off side. He would hit balls which were pitched outside the off stump through the leg side for four when tradition had previously always dictated that a ball bowled on the off side should be *played* on the off side. More recently Kevin Pietersen has become famous for a similar shot and has also become notable as the most successful exponent of the 'switch hit'.

Creative hitting tends to based on one of four principles outlined in the panels below.

OPENING/CLOSING THE FACE OF THE BAT

The effect of this is to change the angle at which the bat contacts the ball. As a result, when well-executed the direction of the ball is altered to beat the field

CLEARING THE FRONT LEG

The traditional technique of placing the front leg towards the line of the ball and playing with a straight bat is today being challenged, as many batters now clear the front leg out of the way deliberately to allow them to swing across the line with the bat at a 45° angle to try and clear the leg-side boundary

CHANGING THE LINE

This is done when the batter moves either to the leg or off side to change their position in relation to the line of the ball. This allows the batter to play a different shot from the one expected by the fielding side

SWITCH HITTING

This involves the batter changing the set-up position at the crease by 180°, effectively 'switching' to the opposite hand (ie, right-handers hitting from a left-handed position and vice versa). Following the switch, the principles of the switch hit tend to be similar to the previous shot, with the front leg being cleared to give access to the ball

Indian batsman Sachin
Tendulkar adopts a low turning
position watched by England
bowler Andrew Flintoff

ENGLAND
CRICKET

RUNNING BETWEEN THE WICKETS

Good running between wickets is the trademark of a well-drilled and effective team that understands and appreciates its importance in the modern game. Running between the wickets has always been an integral part of the game, but recently it has become increasingly important now that every last run is crucial. Training and developing this skill is also receiving more attention, as the standard of fielding has improved significantly in recent years.

When two people are involved in making a series of decisions on a variety of factors when 22 yards apart, there is always the potential for things to go horribly wrong. So in order to run well between the wickets, effective communication and calling is absolutely fundamental. But many other important skills are also required to be an effective runner, including speed, acceleration, effective turning, backing-up by the non-striker, good attitude and awareness. Some of the key points are:

ATTITUDE AND AWARENESS
- Work together as a pair, not as individuals.
- Be aware of each other's speed and ability.
- Look for opportunities to run from every ball.
- Identify gaps, and strong and weak fielders.
- Always pressure the fielders to create an error.
- Run aggressively, looking to convert ones into twos, etc.

BACKING UP AND SETTING OFF
- Non-striker to have the bat in hand nearest the bowler, to face the correct way.
- Stay balanced, ready to move quickly.
- Try not to pre-judge runs or set off too early.
- Move down the pitch towards the other end as the ball is released (not too far).
- Expect to run every ball.
- Be clear with your partner about running lines to avoid collisions.

EFFECTIVE CALLING
- Use clear and simple calls such as, 'Yes!', 'No!', 'Wait!'
- Know and agree whose responsibility it is to call (the striker calls unless their partner has a better view, such as if the ball goes behind the wicket).

- Final responsibility on calls for multiple runs lies with whoever is running to the danger end.
- When called for a run, trust your partner and do not hesitate.

RUNNING AND TURNING
- Take the shortest route, and run in straight lines in pre-agreed lanes.
- Carry the bat in both hands whenever possible (except when stretching for the crease) to improve balance.
- Turn as quickly as possible using low body position to help with braking into and accelerating out of the turn.
- To aid decision-making, always try to turn facing the ball and fielder.
- Ground the bat – either by touching down just behind the line when turning or sliding into the crease when completing the final run.

Ian Bell and
Kevin Pietersen
running hard
between the
wickets

Paul Collingwood
avoids a bouncer
early in an innings

ENGLAND
CRICKET

BUILDING AN INNINGS

For any batter to be consistently successful they must learn how to build an innings. The keys to this are an ability to make good decisions throughout, finding the right balance between attack and defence, and recognising the critical moments at which to apply the tactics that will give the best chance of success.

Traditionally a successful innings started slowly, with the batter being circumspect and defensively minded. This tends to be done to get used to the environment, such as the pace of the pitch, type of bowling, etc. There are also the 'internal' issues that a batter has to deal with, and batters often talk about 'getting their eye in' and 'getting their feet moving'. The ability to leave the ball, particularly early in the innings, is an excellent example of how batters can 'get themselves in'.

As the batter gets more used to the conditions and feels more comfortable that their technique is working well, the pace of run-scoring gradually increases. A batter therefore tends to score more freely towards the end of their innings. This pattern still remains the case today in the longer forms of the game. However, limited-overs cricket, with power plays and artificial fielding restrictions, has encouraged batters to be more aggressive early in

the innings, hitting over and through the infield to take advantage of the opportunities the fielding restrictions present. The batter may then settle into a more risk-free approach, happy to take advantage of the gaps that appear in the infield in the middle of the innings. Then towards the end of the innings, if a batting team has wickets in hand they will up the scoring rate and take more risks in the search for the boundaries that will maximise their total.

As a result of the many differing formats and tactics that are now applied by batting teams, it has become more important for modern batters to be multi-dimensional in their approach. In the past they tended to play only one way, which was very much their preferred style. As a result different types of player would bat at the particular positions in the batting order most likely to suit their style of play, but the modern-day game is more suited to batters who can be comfortable playing several different ways. Players will still have a 'default' style that suits them best, but they must work on developing other batting styles to meet the needs of the team. It is important that batters understand their role within the team, wherever they are asked to bat in the order.

Alastair Cook
leaves the ball
as he attempts
to establish
himself at the
crease

3
BOWLING

ENGLAND CRICKET

INTRODUCTION TO BOWLING

As mentioned earlier, the essence of cricket is the age-old contest between bat and ball. The batters' job is to score as many runs as possible and the bowlers' job is to take wickets and prevent runs from being scored. In the following section we will deal with bowling and the business of taking wickets. Wickets win matches, and bowlers who have a wicket-taking gift are priceless.

It is generally accepted that the best way to take wickets is to do something with the ball that deceives the batter. This is normally done in one of two ways: firstly, by imparting some physical property on the ball to affect 'how' it arrives; and secondly, by landing the ball in an area which creates doubt and uncertainty in the batter's mind regarding 'where' it arrives.

The vast majority of wickets occur when the bowler deceives the batter in one or both of these ways. Sometimes batter error can be entirely responsible for a dismissal, although even when this appears to be the case there is usually some form of deception by the bowler that induces the error. There are many ways in which the properties imparted on the ball can deceive the batter, some of which are very obvious to the eye and some of which are more subtle. The 'big four', however, are pace, spin, swing and seam.

Pace and spin have traditionally been seen as the most effective methods of dismissing a batter. In certain conditions and at certain levels, however, swing through the air and lateral movement off the pitch (caused by the ball landing on its raised seam) can be just as effective.

These key forms of deception have given cricket the terminology and classifications used to describe the different types of bowlers. For the purposes of this manual we will split the bowlers into two general types – 'pace' and 'spin'. We will include seam and swing bowling within the 'pace' section, as even the fastest of bowlers will try to swing and/or move the ball off the seam.

There are, however, many sub-divisions of these different types of bowlers. Pace bowlers, for instance, are often sub-divided by the pace at which they bowl the ball, such as fast, medium fast and medium. Spin bowlers also tend to be sub-divided by the manner in which they spin the ball, with finger spinners and wrist spinners being the two principal categories.

Steve Harmison runs in to bowl

The many different formats of the game now being played have impacted on bowling as much as they have on batting. Many bowlers try to specialise in certain formats, although, like the best batters, the best bowlers tend to be able to apply their skills to all forms of the game. The biggest change that limited-overs cricket has brought to the game has been the need for the bowler to be able to deliver effective variations. Bowling a stock delivery in the same area was for years

seen as the only quality required for success, but this was at a time when a more conservative approach to batting prevailed.

Such conservatism has now been replaced by a much more aggressive approach, and being 'predictable' can lead to a bowler being 'lined up' for boundary hitting. An ability to deliver the stock ball effectively has not become less important, but bowlers have had to become much more adaptable, with more

Shane Warne, the legendary
Australian leg spinner,
retired in 2007 with over
700 test wickets

Muttiah Muralitharan, the Sri
Lankan off spinner, is the leading
wicket taker in test matches and
one-day internationals

ENGLAND
CRICKET

variations at their disposal; and an ability to deliver these variations consistently has become even more crucial, as getting it wrong can often be costly in terms of runs conceded. Yet despite these tactical developments and the increased demands of the modern game, the fundamental principles of bowling have changed little over the years.

Throughout the history of cricket, the most successful bowlers have been the ones who have combined a potent threat of deception with unerring accuracy. Legends of the game in recent memory are pace bowlers such as Dennis Lillee, Michael Holding, Courtney Walsh, Alan Donald and Brett Lee; spin bowlers such as Bishan Bedi, Abdul Qadir, Shane Warne and Muttiah Muralitharan; and swing and seam bowlers like Richard Hadlee, Wasim Akram and Glenn McGrath.

In the following pages we will explore the general principles of bowling and the techniques that have made such players so successful. It is important to bear in mind that everyone is different and that the bowling action, more than any other discipline in cricket, is highly individualised to each player. This is principally due to each individual's unique physical make-up. The truly great bowlers throughout history have generally attained their status by adhering to several key technical principles while at the same time adding something of their individual talent and flair.

By taking the timeless principles of bowling and adapting them to the needs of the modern game, we arrive at the following conclusions, which hold true for aspiring young bowlers and the coaches who help them to develop:

■ Successful bowlers are those able to deceive the batter by influencing the behaviour of the ball and 'how' it arrives, while exercising judgement and control over line and length and 'where' it arrives.

■ Greater scientific study and the use of biomechanical principles have underpinned the need to teach a core set of technical principles which help bowlers become effective, while at the same time accepting and embracing the individual differences that can provide the 'x factor' and enable bowlers to become successful.

Laura Marsh appeals
during the 2009 ICC
Women's World Cup final
against New Zealand

ENGLAND
CRICKET

BASICS OF BOWLING

Taking wickets is the most important skill that any bowler can possess. If bowlers can do this while conceding as few runs as possible, they become doubly valuable to the teams.

The need to be economical has been intensified by limited-overs cricket. In this format economical bowling has become more important than taking wickets. The job of taking wickets, however, is made easier for any bowler if they have good control of where and how they land the ball on the pitch. The key to where the ball lands is dictated by the bowler's ability to control the line of the ball in relation to the batter and stumps, and the length of the ball and how far it lands from the batter. This control of line and length makes the batter's job of scoring runs much more difficult and as a result increases the bowler's chances of taking wickets.

If taking wickets is the priority, then the bowler should try to induce the batter into playing a stroke. Ideally this would be a ball of a line and length that creates some doubt in the batter's mind and one that is difficult to score from. These factors vastly increase the bowler's chances of taking a wicket.

The ideal line and length varies for different types of bowlers and is also dependent upon many other different factors, as given in the panel below.

There are, however, many key principles that remain consistent with regard to both line and length for all bowlers. Over the next few pages we will consider the principles of both line and length. This will be done separately, to allow for clarity in the description of each, but it must be stressed that the concepts of both line and length are complementary and should be considered together.

Kabir Ali of Worcestershire gets his line and length right as he removes the batter's off stump

KEY FACTORS

- Whether the bowling is from over or round the wicket (different sides of the stumps)

- The type of delivery being bowled

- Whether the batter is left- or right-handed

- The height and reach of the batter

- The preferred style of the batter

- The state of the game

- The type of wicket (wet or dry, fast or slow, etc)

**Andrew Flintoff bowls
a challenging line in the
'corridor of uncertainty'**

BOWLING LINE

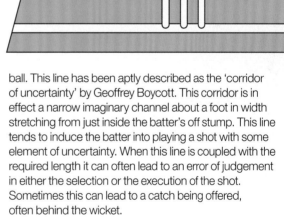

The line of a cricket ball when bowled is the direction in which it is travelling measured against an imaginary line drawn along the length of the pitch from one set of stumps to the other. The variations in line are referred to in terms of the line of the ball in relation to the stumps. For example, an off-side line would be one that is outside off stump, while a leg-stump line would be aimed in the general direction of leg stump.

Note that our diagram shows the ideal line for a right-arm bowler, bowling over the wicket to a right-handed batter. The terms 'over' and 'round' the wicket denote which side of the stumps the ball is being bowled from. Right arm over the wicket is bowled from the left of the stumps (as shown). Alternatively right arm round is bowled from the right-hand side. The opposite applies for a left-armer, with over the wicket being to the right, and round being from the left.

The line tends to control which shots a batter is able to play. For example, an accomplished batter will tend to be able to play free-scoring attacking shots to deliveries on or outside leg stump and similarly to those well wide of off stump. Therefore a bowler would not look to bowl either of those lines on a regular basis for fear of conceding too many runs and being withdrawn from the attack by the captain. It is important to remember that the captain will always have a range of choices of who to bowl. Bowlers need to be bowling to take wickets, so consistency is important if a bowler is to feature regularly and take wickets.

Sometimes bowlers will bowl a 'straight' line, which is often referred to as 'wicket to wicket' due to the direction of the ball towards the stumps. This tactic is a direct form of attacking bowling that can often result in the batter being dismissed by being bowled or leg before wicket if the ball is missed by the bat. This type of delivery also increases the chances of the batter being caught, as it demands that a stroke of some sort is played to avoid one of the previous two forms of dismissal.

Despite the obvious appeal of this more direct tactic, most accomplished batters are comfortable with the ball bowled directly at the stumps and can, depending on conditions, find these deliveries relatively easy to score off. As a result most bowlers will concentrate their efforts on bowling a line on or just outside the accomplished batter's off stump. In general this is an ideal line as the batter is unsure whether or not they need to play at the ball. This line has been aptly described as the 'corridor of uncertainty' by Geoffrey Boycott. This corridor is in effect a narrow imaginary channel about a foot in width stretching from just inside the batter's off stump. This line tends to induce the batter into playing a shot with some element of uncertainty. When this line is coupled with the required length it can often lead to an error of judgement in either the selection or the execution of the shot. Sometimes this can lead to a catch being offered, often behind the wicket.

Bowling a particular line can also be used as a deliberate tactic by a fielding team. The aim of this tactic is to frustrate the opposing batters with the use of well-set fields. For example, bowling a line consistently wide of off stump to a heavily loaded off-side field has been used with great success by teams in both limited-overs cricket and the longer forms of the game.

The ability to bowl any one of these attacking lines is dependent on a bowler's skill in letting the ball go in the desired direction. This is done through a consistent sequence of body movements (known as the bowling action) that direct the ball towards the chosen target line.

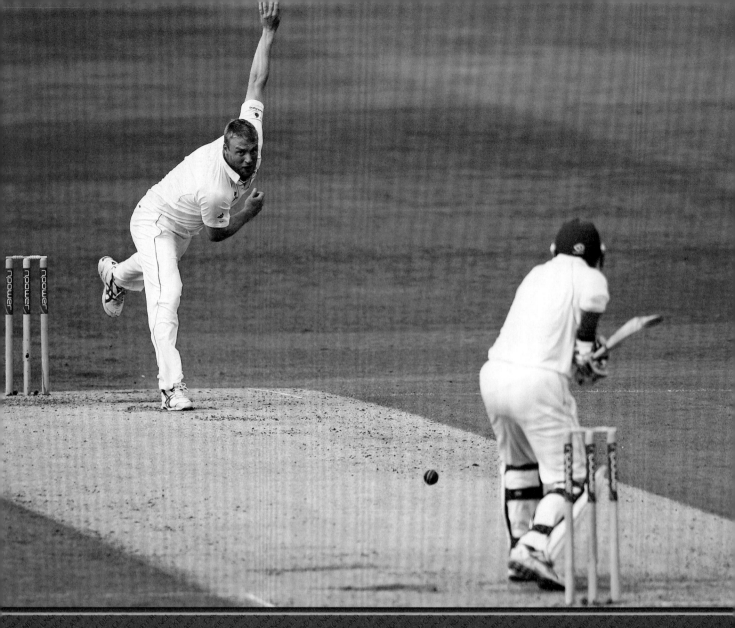

BOWLING LENGTH

Andrew Flintoff bowls a good length delivery which draws the batter forward

The length of a delivery is judged by the distance the ball lands from the stumps at the opposite end. In cricket terms there tend to be five classifications applied to a length of delivery. These are:

- Full toss
- Half volley/full length
- Good length
- Short/back of a length
- Bouncer/long hop

The length of the ball dictates how high it will rise from the pitch after bouncing. A short-pitched ball will generally lose pace and rise higher as it reaches the batter. Unless bowled at extreme pace (a bouncer)

this tends to give the batter a good sight of the line and bounce of the ball, making shot selection and execution easier. A fuller-pitched ball, which pitches closer to the batter, has less time and distance to deviate sideways or rise to any significant height, again making it easier for the batter to select and execute the chosen shot. There are, nevertheless, always exceptions to the rule and sometimes a fuller-pitched ball that swings late in the air can still deceive a batter into a false shot. This, however, tends to apply to a fuller ball that is erring towards a good-length delivery.

The lengths that tend to cause the batter most problems are the in-between ones. A good-length ball bounces far enough from the batter for it to deviate significantly off the straight, but not so far away for

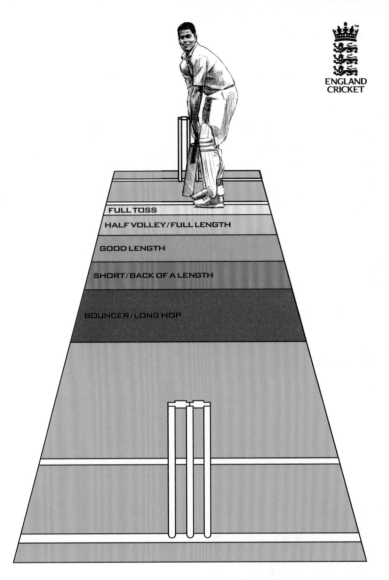

the deviation to be accurately assessed. This creates doubt and uncertainty for the batter, and as we have seen in the section on line, such emotions are the bowler's friends. These doubts can often lead to poor shot selection or execution by the batter, thus increasing the chance of them being dismissed.

A good length is dependent on a variety of circumstances, such as:

- The pace of the bowler
- The pace of the pitch
- The type of delivery being bowled
- The height and reach of the batter
- The preferred style of the batter
- The state of the game

The pace of the bowler and pitch are crucial to the judgement of a good length. A hard, fast-paced pitch will normally demand a shorter length, while a softer, slower pitch will require a fuller length to be bowled. A good length for a male adult pace bowler on a good hard pitch tends to measure approximately 6–8m from the popping crease and batter. A swing bowler or slower medium-paced bowler would have to pitch the ball slightly fuller than this on a good pitch to bowl that 'doubt-creating' length. Similarly, a good length for an adult male spin bowler on a good pitch would be 3–4.5m from the bat. It is important to remember that determining the perfect length for a bowler is far from being an exact science, and will vary for a wide variety of reasons.

Bowling a particular length can also be used as a deliberate tactic by a bowler. The aim of this tactic is to set up the batter by the consistent use of one length of delivery. Having thereby established a pattern for the batter, a 'change-up' length of delivery is then bowled in order to surprise and disturb the batter's rhythm. For example, a pace bowler may choose to bowl consistently short-pitched balls to push a batter on to the back foot, before slipping in a fuller, straighter ball. This is designed to catch them unawares with their weight on the back foot. This can often result in a false shot played from a poor position, and increases the chances of the batter being out-bowled or leg before wicket.

COMBINING LINE AND LENGTH

While it is important to understand the separate principles of both line and length, it is equally important to understand that when applying them in a bowling context they need to be considered together. Bowling a consistently good line is no guarantee of success if the lengths are poor. Similarly, bowling a good length with a poor line will not make a bowler consistently successful.

Creating uncertainty in the mind of the batter by repeatedly putting the ball in their least-desired area is fundamental to a bowler's chances of success. This is done by making accurate assessments of the batter, good decisions on the line and length required, and having the technical ability to deliver the ball consistently in the chosen area.

How the ball arrives and the quality of the deception comprise the second factor that will help bowlers to take wickets. These skills do, however, become far less effective if the bowler cannot deliver a consistent line and length. To achieve this a bowler must have confidence in the repeatability of their bowling action. As mentioned earlier, each bowling action is unique to the individual, but there is nevertheless a set of fundamental principles that tend to give bowlers the best chance of success. In the following sections we will examine these principles for both pace and spin bowling.

PACE BOWLING EXPLAINED

The bowling action has evolved significantly during the history of cricket, from the under-arm and round-arm techniques of the 18th and early 19th centuries to the over-arm version we know today. A simple physical explanation of the bowling action would describe it as a straight bowling arm rotating vertically around the shoulder joint to impart forces on the ball that propel it towards the target. A 'straight' bowling arm is now defined as one that may flex at the elbow to a limit of 15° from straight. However, bowlers should attempt to bowl with their arm fully extended in order to prevent the risk of 'throwing', which is deemed to be an illegal delivery.

The bowling actions we know today are a highly complex sequence of movements that have evolved over the years in order to give bowlers the best chance of creating deception and achieving consistency.

The bowling action is a very fluid and rhythmical movement, and is also very complex. It is important, therefore, to be able to simplify it. This can be done by breaking it down into several key phases, which allow us to see what a good technical model may look like at each stage.

The bowling action must also be supported by the correct grip. There are many different types of delivery in cricket and as a result many different grips. This manual will explain the preferred grip for each type of delivery. It is important to understand that the grip is fundamental to the desired outcome of the action.

In addition to the basic grip for pace bowling there are six key phases of the bowling action and these are shown over the next three pages.

THE BASIC GRIP

There are many variations on the grip for a pace bowler. The basic grip, however. is as follows:

- Seam vertical
- Side of thumb on seam underneath ball
- Index and middle fingers on either side of seam

NB It is important to recognise that the following are general technical principles and that some bowlers may not adhere to all of them. The integrity of each individual bowling action should always be protected while recognising that the principles mentioned generally help develop and improve performance.

THE KEY CRITERIA FOR A SUCCESSFUL PACE BOWLER

To achieve the desired result of taking wickets and stopping runs, a pace bowler should either possess or be developing the following characteristics:

- A potent threat through pace, swing or seam
- A set of effective variations
- Control and consistency
- Tactical awareness
- Physical fitness
- Mental strength

These characteristics are greatly aided by the following:

Good alignment of the bowling action towards the target
A strong and repeatable action
Commitment and a strong work ethic

ENGLAND
CRICKET

Andrew Flintoff
runs in

James Anderson jumps into
his delivery stride

RUN-UP/APPROACH

The type of approach will vary significantly depending on the speed and style of the bowler. In general the run-up should be smooth, balanced, rhythmical and consistent.

- Starting with small steps, the stride pattern lengthens during approach
- A slight forward lean on the run-up
- Arms stay close to body through the run-up
- Hands keep moving consistent with efficient running motion towards the target
- Head remains steady and upright with eyes fixed on target

JUMP AND GATHER

This is effectively the transition phase from the run-up into the delivery stride. The nature of this phase varies, depending on whether the bowler prefers a more side-on or front-on delivery style.

- The feet follow a normal running pattern
- The arms remain as close to the body as possible
- Momentum should remain towards target
- The body turns in the air as appropriate to the preferred bowling style
- Head and body remain upright through transition

James Anderson lands in
a side-on position

Andrew Flintoff in
delivery stride

PRE-DELIVERY

This is when the back foot makes contact with the ground prior to establishing the 'bowling base'.

- Back foot lands consistent with preferred bowling style (eg, foot lands side-on for side-on action)
- Back leg remains stable to support the body
- Body remains upright and moving towards the target
- Hands and arms remain close to the body within width of shoulders
- Head remains steady and upright

DELIVERY STRIDE

This is the point where the front foot lands, creating the solid 'bowling base' that helps propel the ball towards the target.

- Front and back foot landing points are generally aligned towards target
- Front leg stabilises and prepares to support the shoulder rotation
- Arms and shoulders rotate vertically towards the target
- Head remains steady and upright

ENGLAND
CRICKET

Stuart Broad
releases the ball

Stuart Broad in his
follow-through

RELEASE

FOLLOW-THROUGH

The point where the bowler lets go of the ball towards the intended target area, with momentum transferring forwards towards the target.

- The ball is released close to the highest point of the delivery arc
- Body remains as upright as possible on release
- Fingers and wrist in appropriate position (normally behind ball) for the desired delivery
- Front arm remains close to the body at point of release
- Head remains steady and as upright as possible

The ball has been released and momentum has been transferred over the front leg towards the target.

- Body continues to move towards target (avoiding restricted zone in front of the stumps)
- Shoulder rotation continues, completing 180° vertical rotation
- Bowling arm finishes off movement in general across body
- Front arm releases behind body
- Head remains upright and fixed on ball

TYPES OF BOWLING ACTIONS

As has already been stated, every bowling action is unique to each individual as a result of their different physical attributes and movement patterns. There are, however, three recognised types of bowling action for pace bowlers. These are:

- Side-on
- Front-on
- Midway

These three classifications relate to the position of the body in relation to the target at back and front foot contact through the delivery stride.

Up until about 30 years ago all bowlers were coached to bowl from a side-on position. Australian fast bowling legend Dennis Lillee would be a classic example of an old-fashioned side-on fast bowler.

Then, in the 1980s, a crop of West Indian pace bowlers became very successful bowling with a more front-on, open-chested action. At this point it was recognised that there was more than one effective style for pace bowlers. As a result, coaches are now far more comfortable coaching bowlers who prefer a more front-on style. The West Indian pace duo of Courtney Walsh and Curtly Ambrose are obvious examples of highly successful front-on bowlers.

Even more recently a new classification of 'midway' has emerged. This type of bowler is one who bowls from neither a side-on nor a front-on position, but from somewhere between the two. This tends to be at about a 45° angle, hence the term midway. South African fast bowler Alan Donald is an excellent example of a midway bowling style.

Every young bowler should be encouraged to follow their natural tendency when it comes to back-foot contact, with the coach's job being to ensure the shoulders and hips align to maintain a safe bowling action. When the hips and shoulders are out of alignment the action is deemed to be mixed, and the bowler risks serious injury. More information on mixed actions is available in the section on injury prevention.

The three different type of actions are explained in the accompanying panels.

SIDE-ON ACTION

In a side-on action the back foot lands parallel to the crease, aligning the hips and the shoulders in a sideways position in relation to the target. This allows for a 180° shoulder and hip rotation towards the target. It tends to be more comfortable for the majority of young bowlers, who are still usually introduced to bowling from a side-on base position. Indeed, the majority of bowlers still use a side-on action, and it is consequently sometimes referred to as the 'classic' bowling action.

Ryan Sidebottom lands side-on

FRONT-ON ACTION

In a front-on action the back foot lands perpendicular to the crease, pointing down the wicket towards the batter. This leaves the bowler's body in a front-on position, their shoulders aligned with their hips and their chest towards the target. This allows the bowler to run through their action more, with a reduced bound, which in turn helps maintain momentum towards the target. To be effective, this action tends to require a good degree of flexibility in the shoulder joint.

Stuart Broad lands front-on

MIDWAY ACTION

A midway action is one in which the back foot lands at an angle of approximately 45° to the crease. The hips and shoulders should then be aligned at the same angle to the target. This enables a midway bowler to maintain more momentum towards the target than a side-on bowler but less than a front-on bowler. It also allows them to gain more hip and shoulder rotation than a front-on bowler but less than a side-on.

Steve Kirby lands midway

PACE BOWLING

INJURY PREVENTION

Steve Harmison feels the pain of a knee injury

The welfare of pace bowlers and the prevention of injuries, particularly for developing young bowlers, is an ongoing concern for the cricketing authorities. There are three main areas that tend be the biggest causes of injury in young pace bowlers:

- Mixed bowling actions
- Poor physical conditioning
- Over-bowling

MIXED BOWLING ACTIONS

These occur when the hips and shoulders are misaligned at front-foot contact. An example would be the front-on mixed action, which occurs when the back foot lands pointing towards the batter but the upper body turns into a side-on position. This misalignment causes a twisting of the spine at front-foot contact and can be extremely harmful. The solution has been the education of coaches and young players regarding the dangers of mixed actions, and the promotion of 'good' alignment. Hence the following top tip from the ECB Coach Education Manual: **'Keep the hips and shoulders in line and you will be fine: twist the back and it will crack'**.

POOR PHYSICAL CONDITIONING

It has long been known that many young bowlers, especially maturing teenagers, are not strong enough to endure the physical demands of pace bowling. This can sometimes manifest itself in knee and ankle injuries due to the stresses being placed on the joints on both back and

ENGLAND
CRICKET

front-foot contact. However, the most common and worrying injury attributed to poor conditioning is again to the back.

A lack of core strength and the inability to maintain an upright position through the delivery stride can lead to excessive lateral flexion of the back. In simple terms the spine bends too far sideways, creating a crushing pressure on the side of the vertebrae in the lower back. The answer to this problem is to improve core strength through both dynamic and static strengthening exercises and to improve overall strength throughout the length of the body.

OVER-BOWLING

One of the unusual things about cricket is the tradition of playing day after day during what is quite a short summer in the northern hemisphere. This tends to have particular impact on talented young pace bowlers, who are often in great demand at many levels. They may play one or two days a week for the club junior teams, one or two days with the club senior team and possibly another day or two with a representative side. Most people would agree that bowling six or seven days a week is not a good way to prevent injury in a young fast bowler who is still growing. As a result the ECB has introduced fast bowling directives for young cricketers. These are designed to give coaches and administrators a guide to reasonable workloads for young pace bowlers. For example, under the directives a 15-year-old would be restricted to three matches or practice sessions in a week, and should bowl

no more than two spells of five overs in a match or 36 balls in a practice session. It should be noted that these directives are for guidance only and while adhered to in recognised competitions they are sometimes less well respected elsewhere.

SUMMARY OF ECB DIRECTIVES

Directives for matches		
Age	Maximum per spell	Maximum per day
U13	4 overs	8 overs
U14, U15	5 overs	10 overs
U16, U17	6 overs	18 overs
U19	7 overs	21 overs
Directive for practice sessions		
Age	Maximum per session	Sessions per week
U13	30 deliveries	2
U14, U15	36 deliveries	2
U16, U17	37 deliveries	3
U19	42 deliveries	3

The key lesson regarding injuries, especially to young bowlers, is that greater understanding is required among both coaches and players about the nature and potential effect of the stresses placed on the body by pace bowling. There is also a need to be pro-active regarding the prevention and avoidance of injury in young bowlers. Once a bowler gets hurt, the chance of such injuries recurring increases significantly. The best approach for a young pace bowler is to prevent the injury from occurring in the first place.

England players do shoulder-strengthening exercises during their warm-up

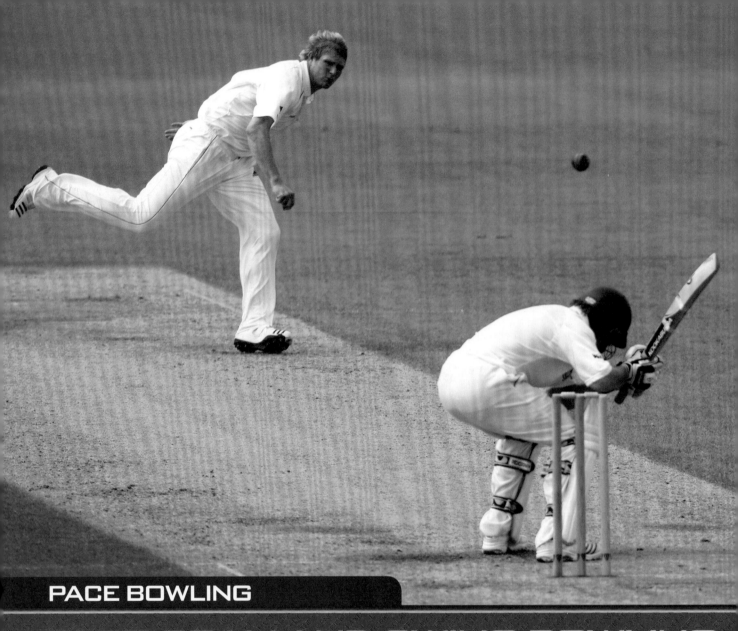

PACE BOWLING

FAST, SEAM AND SWING BOWLING

Mathew Hoggard bowls a bouncer

Seam and swing bowling are both effectively sub-divisions of pace bowling. The different terms used to describe bowlers can sometimes be confusing, but they have traditionally been utilised as a means of identifying a particular bowler's perceived strength or specialisation. For example, Andrew Flintoff tends to be classified as a fast bowler, even though he utilises both seam and swing to try and get wickets.

These days the term 'fast bowler', in the context of the men's professional game, tends to be reserved for those who bowl close to or in excess of 90mph – though what is deemed 'fast' in other situations will vary greatly depending on the standard and age of the participants. Fast bowlers are in effect seam and swing

bowlers who possess the additional gift of speed. Other speed classifications include fast-medium bowlers (who tend to bowl well in excess of 80mph) and medium-pace bowlers (who tend to bowl at less than or around 80mph), and it is these latter two categories who tend to be labelled as specialist 'seam' or 'swing' bowlers. England's Matthew Hoggard would be a good example of a player generally categorised as a medium-pace swing bowler.

SEAM BOWLING

All pace bowlers, irrespective of their chosen speciality, normally bowl with the ball's seam upright, which is known in cricketing terminology as 'seam up'.

The simple definition of seam bowling is when the

ENGLAND CRICKET

ball is deliberately bowled to land on the seam, which causes it to deviate slightly from its original path. This deviation tends to be lateral (sideways) but can occasionally be longitudinal, which is reflected in how high the ball bounces. Such movement means that there is more chance of the ball deceiving the batter, especially given that they have only the brief moment following the ball's bounce to assess its direction.

The reason that the ball behaves in this way is to do with its composition. A cricket ball is not a perfect sphere. Its leather covering is made up of four quarters that are finely stitched into two halves and then used to tightly cover the core of the ball and stitched together. This stitching creates a protruding seam, which travels round the whole circumference of the ball. The resultant irregularity of its surface is what causes the ball to deviate.

The direction and degree of deviation from the straight are dependent on how much or which part of the seam lands directly on the pitch. The condition of the pitch at the landing point will also have an effect on the subsequent behaviour of the ball after it has bounced.

SWING BOWLING

The simplest definition of swing bowling is when a ball is bowled in a way that enables it to alter its line through the air in a curving motion. This swing either occurs inwards towards the batter or alternatively away from the batter. Generally the later the ball

swings, the better it is for the bowler. This gives the batter less time to assess where and how the ball will arrive. The explanation of what makes the ball swing is complex and quite scientific, but remembering the key points in the accompanying panel will aid understanding.

SWING BOWLING
KEY FACTORS

■ Air flows round both sides of the ball as it travels towards the batter, and the ball swings when there is an imbalance in the type of airflow around each side

■ The ball will always swing towards the side with the more turbulent airflow

In essence there are four physical factors which can help create the aforementioned imbalance and encourage the ball to swing:

■ The differing condition of each side of the ball

■ The angle at which the raised seam is presented

■ The bowler's action

■ The speed at which the ball is delivered

James Anderson takes off in his follow through

Ryan Sidebottom bowls South Africa's Jacques Kallis with an in-swinging Yorker

CONVENTIONAL SWING

The differing condition of each side of the ball is encouraged by the fielding side deliberately affecting it. This is normally achieved by the constant polishing of one side of the ball as it gets older, most often by the application of a small amount of moisture (usually sweat or saliva) followed by vigorous rubbing against an item of clothing (usually the upper thigh of the trousers). The other side of the ball is meanwhile allowed to wear naturally through impact with the bat and ground. This causes an imbalance in the surface of the ball, with one side shiny and polished and the other side much rougher.

This imbalance produces a marked difference in the aerodynamic properties of each side of the ball. The shiny side encourages a smooth airflow, while the rougher side has a more turbulent airflow, thus creating the imbalance that encourages the ball to swing towards the rough side and away from the shiny side. Therefore if a bowler wishes to swing the ball from right to left as they would see it travel (an out-swinger to a right-hander) they would present an upright seam with the shiny side to the right on its direction of travel. The opposite would apply if the bowler wished to swing the ball from left to right.

Note that this explanation applies to conventional swing bowling and may appear to be contradicted by a newer phenomenon known as 'reverse swing'. There is, however, a scientific explanation for this, and it is covered in the section on reverse swing.

The raised seam itself and the angle at which it is presented can also bring about the desired imbalance that causes swing, by creating a turbulent airflow behind it. A bowler wishing to swing the ball from right to left would therefore present the seam angled slightly to the left, to create more turbulence on the left-hand side of the ball. Since the ball swings towards the side with more turbulence, it would therefore swing to the left. The opposite would be the case if the bowler wished to swing the ball to the right. This is what enables a new ball to swing when there is as yet no imbalance in the condition of either side.

The nature of the bowler's action can also influence how well the seam is presented, and the correct sequence of body movements can help influence the path of the ball. More will be said about this in the following section, which includes in- and out-swing.

The speed of the ball is another factor that can influence how much it swings. Science tells us that at around 80mph (medium pace) the airflow around the ball is more smooth (the scientific term is 'laminar') than at 90mph (fast), when the airflow is much more turbulent. The smooth airflow round the shiny side of the ball helps cause the airflow differential that makes it swing. Therefore it is easier for a medium-pace bowler to swing the ball. The quicker bowlers can still swing the ball, but not to the same extent, due to the turbulent nature of the airflow round both sides of the ball.

The fact that several factors often combine to make the ball swing makes swing bowling a somewhat inexact science, with a bit of trial and error being required to find the optimum swing on any given day. Although beyond the bowler's control, weather conditions also appear to affect the likelihood of the ball swinging. Cloudy and humid conditions generally accentuate conventional swing due to the 'heavier' and 'damper' nature of the air.

REVERSE SWING

Unfortunately, as was alluded to earlier, it is also necessary to understand the concept of 'reverse swing', which can potentially confuse matters. It was first used knowingly as a tactic around 20 years ago, and has its origins in the Indian sub-continent, where conventional out-swing bowling tended to be largely ineffective because the shine wore off the ball more quickly due to the abrasive nature of the playing surfaces. As the condition of the ball deteriorated further and the 'neglected' side became extremely scuffed, the ball would appear to defy convention and swing towards the *smoother* side when bowled at high speed. Pakistan's Waqar Younis is arguably the first

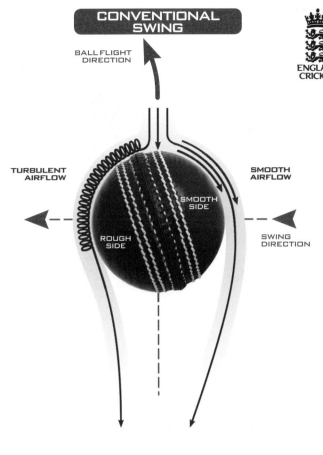

CONVENTIONAL SWING

BALL FLIGHT DIRECTION

TURBULENT AIRFLOW

SMOOTH AIRFLOW

SMOOTH SIDE

ROUGH SIDE

SWING DIRECTION

expert in the art of reversing the direction of swing. Since this reverse-swing phenomenon appears to contradict the principles of conventional swing, a further understanding of science is required in order to explain it.

Given that the ball will always swing towards the side with more turbulent airflow, logic demands that different conditions must be created in order for there to be more turbulence on the smoother side of the ball. The four factors that appear to combine to help a ball to reverse swing are given in the panel below.

The result of a combination of these four factors would appear to be enough to reverse the airflow imbalance and for the ball to swing towards the smoother side (see the diagrams to the right).

Reverse swing has become a much-used tactic at the elite end of the game, where the best fast bowlers operate. It is a devastating weapon in a pace bowler's armoury due to the late and prodigious amount of swing it tends to produce. It is particularly (although not exclusively) effective when a right-arm fast bowler using a conventional out-swing grip is able to bowl unplayable, full-length, 90mph deliveries swinging late in towards the right-hand batter's stumps. England fast bowlers Andrew Flintoff, Steve Harmison and Simon Jones used this tactic to devastating effect in the Ashes series of 2005.

REVERSE SWING
KEY FACTORS

- At 90mph the airflow around both sides of the ball is more turbulent, thus negating the airflow differential that promotes conventional swing

- The severe deterioration on one side of the ball allied to a damp 'smooth' side rather than a 'shiny' side appears to create more turbulence on the smoother side, thus reversing the conventional theory

- The presentation of the seam at a slightly tilted angle can help create more turbulent airflow towards the smoother side of the ball

- A more 'slingy', open-chested action, with a lower arm action, promotes a more advantageous seam position and encourages movement more in-swing than out-swing in nature

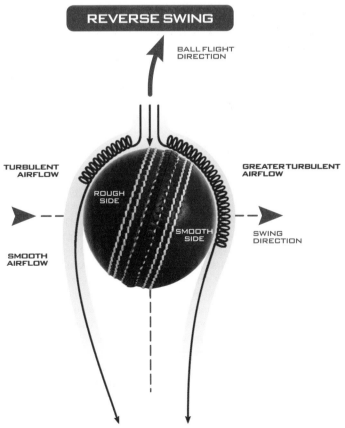

REVERSE SWING

BALL FLIGHT DIRECTION

TURBULENT AIRFLOW

GREATER TURBULENT AIRFLOW

ROUGH SIDE

SMOOTH SIDE

SMOOTH AIRFLOW

SWING DIRECTION

DIFFERENT DELIVERIES

England swing and seam bowler James Anderson bowls to a loaded slip cordon

The science underpinning both seam and swing bowling is useful in explaining why the ball will behave in a way that will be helpful to the bowler. The bowler, however, still needs to know what type of deliveries to use and how to execute them effectively. The grip on the ball and the sequence of body movements through the bowling action are the tools at the bowler's disposal to help them swing or seam the ball.

Bowlers have many different deliveries at their disposal to try and dismiss the batter. Sometimes a single delivery is enough to deceive the batter and capture the wicket. At other times the bowler will need to use a tactical sequence of deliveries to try and dismiss the batter. As was highlighted by the relatively recent advent of reverse swing, bowlers are constantly trying to devise new ways to take wickets. This section of the book is dedicated to the different types of delivery used in the modern game. It also examines the ideal grip on the ball, the key principles involved in the delivery, and the desired path the ball should follow.

In order to avoid confusion, the following explanations assume that the delivery is being bowled by a right-arm bowler bowling over the wicket to a right-handed batter. These principles are, however, entirely transferable to a left-arm bowler. The terminology does change when there is a right- and left-handed combination of batter and bowler, but the principles always remain the same.

SEAMER

BOUNCER

YORKER

In order to land the ball on the seam, the bowler must release the ball with the seam upright. This is not as simple as it might sound and is dependent on the consistency of the bowler's action. This should closely replicate the basic bowling action described on pages 90–91. Further key components include a good basic grip and a cocked wrist locked directly behind the ball to help propel it straight out of the hand. The fingers should also roll down the back of the ball prior to release, creating a backward rotation that keeps the alignment of the seam upright. This gives the ball the best chance of landing on the seam and deviating off the straight, thereby improving the bowler's chances of getting a wicket.

This is one of several variations available to the pace bowler. The bouncer is a delivery that is deliberately pitched far enough short of a length that it rises up to shoulder or head height. The bowler does this by letting go of the ball later than normal, thus altering the trajectory so that it bounces earlier and far enough away from the batter to rise to the desired height. This delivery has three potential uses for the pace bowler:

- ■ To physically and mentally intimidate the batter and let them know that they could potentially get hurt
- ■ To prevent run-scoring, as the batter's attacking options are limited
- ■ To tempt the batter into playing a false shot that may result in a catch

The bouncer should only be used on a firm surface and by bowlers who can bowl quickly enough for it to be a danger to the batter when it arrives. A ball travelling slowly towards a batter at shoulder height tends to be easy to hit. A slow delivery of this type is known as a 'long hop', for obvious reasons.

This variation is the opposite of the bouncer. The Yorker is a full-length delivery designed to pitch on or near the popping crease. This tactic is designed to take the batter by surprise. When directed towards the stumps it can often sneak under the bat of the surprised batter, resulting in them being bowled. Alternatively it can hit the batter's foot, resulting in them being given out LBW. The bowler achieves this by releasing the ball slightly earlier than normal, thus altering the trajectory so that it bounces later and close to the batter. An accurate Yorker is one of the most devastating wicket-taking deliveries in cricket.

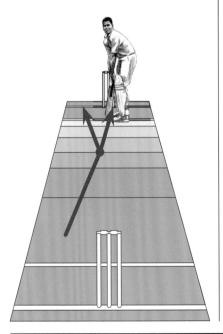

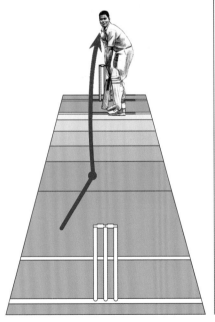

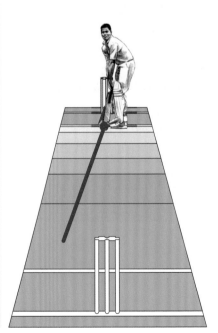

OFF-CUTTER

For this delivery a right-handed bowler uses their index finger to pull across and down the right-hand side of the ball (left-hand side for a left-handed bowler). This action is similar to bowling an off-break such as a spin bowler would bowl, only quicker. From the right-arm bowler's perspective, this makes the ball deviate slightly from left to right after it pitches. This ball is often used as an alternative or 'change-up' tactic by a bowler who naturally moves the ball away from the right-hander. The off-cutter then becomes a surprise delivery that angles back towards the stumps, often bowling or trapping the batter LBW.

LEG-CUTTER

This delivery is the opposite of the off-cutter. For a leg-cutter the right-handed bowler uses his middle finger to pull across and down the left-hand side of the ball (right-hand side for a left-handed bowler). This has a similar outcome to leg-break delivery bowled by a wrist-spin bowler, but at a greater speed. From the right-arm bowler's perspective this makes the ball deviate from right to left after it pitches. The deviation of a leg-cutter is not as much as a leg-break, but at higher speeds it can be enough to either catch the edge of the bat or assist the batter in misjudging a drive and being caught.

OUT-SWINGER

This delivery uses the principles described in the previous section on swing bowling. To bowl an out-swinger, a right-handed bowler will present an upright seam at an angle pointing slightly to the left of the intended path of the ball when released. This is normally combined with placing the smoother, more polished side of the ball to the right and the rougher, more neglected side to the left. This will encourage the ball to swing to the left.

The out-swing bowler's action is to all intents and purposes the same as the standard bowling action for the pace bowler. However, specialist swing bowlers have traditionally tended to deliver using a slightly lower bowling arm to encourage the away movement from the right-hander. Like the leg-cutter, the out-swinger will tend to dismiss batters by getting them caught behind the wicket while playing a defensive shot, or on the off side in front of the wicket as a result of a mistimed drive.

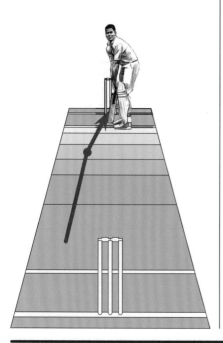

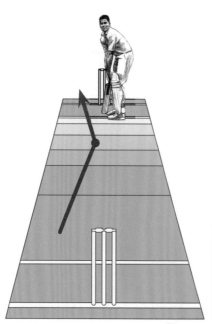

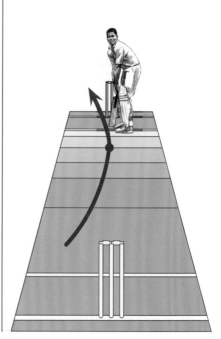

IN-SWINGER   REVERSE SWING   SLOWER BALLS

This is the opposite delivery to an out-swinger. An in-swinger is bowled by a right-handed bowler by presenting an upright seam at an angle pointing slightly to the right of the intended path of the ball on release. This is normally combined with placing the smoother, more polished side to the left and the rougher, more neglected side to the right. This will encourage the ball to swing to the right. The in-swing bowling action should be as similar to the basic pace bowler's action as possible, although a slightly more open-chested action with a high delivery arm following through on the same side and not across the body will encourage in-swing.

Some bowlers use the in-swinger as their stock delivery, but this rarely happens at elite level today. Instead it is more often used as an alternative to the out-swinger. Like the off-cutter, it is frequently used as a surprise or 'change-up' ball that swings back towards the stumps, often bowling or trapping the batter LBW.

As explained earlier, reverse swing is a phenomenon that makes the ball swing in the opposite direction to conventional swing. Its most common use is when a right-arm fast bowler makes an older ball reverse by placing its extremely deteriorated side to the left and the smoother surface to the right. This would traditionally have been thought to be a conventional out-swinger, but by tilting the seam position with a lower arm and a more 'slingy', open-chested action, the ball will now swing in towards a right-handed batter.

The characteristics that make reverse swing such a potent weapon are late prodigious swing and pace (reverse swing only tends to occur at a pace approaching or in excess of 90mph when the ball is of full or Yorker length). In addition to this, the cues the batter picks up tend to make them expect the ball to be a conventional out-swinger. This makes them even less prepared for late in-swing and often results in the batter being bowled or out LBW.

There are many varieties of slower ball now being used by the pace bowler. Such deliveries have become much more common with the rise of one-day and Twenty 20 cricket. They tend to be highly individual to each bowler and are often developed through trial and error in practice. Some bowlers use a slower off- or leg-cutter, some bowl the ball from deep in the hand or even completely out of the back of the hand. The main purpose of the slower ball is to deceive the batter, who, thinking that it is coming at its normal pace, is encouraged to play their chosen shot earlier than they need to, resulting in a catch.

There are also other slow deliveries that the pace bowler can use to deceive the batter, such as varying the angle of delivery on the crease and bowling over and round the wicket. It is also important to remember that, as the human body is not a perfect machine, each delivery will have a degree of natural variation.

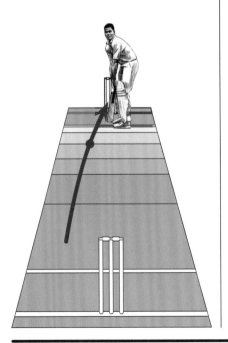

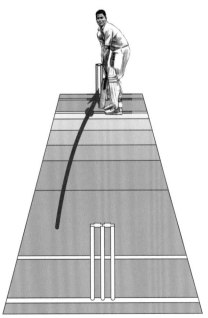

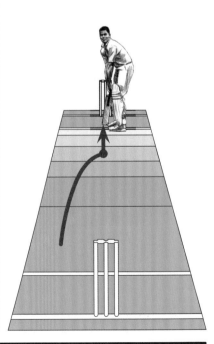

SETTING FIELDS FOR PACE

Cricket has changed dramatically in the past decade in relation to setting fields for pace bowlers. There are now three distinctly different formats of the game, more variations are being used by bowlers, and differing tactics are being used by both batters and bowlers. This has made the setting of fields much more flexible and the changing of fields far more frequent. Two examples of fields set for pace bowlers are shown here.

AN ATTACKING FIELD SET FOR A PACE BOWLER AT THE START OF A MATCH

FINE LEG

SLIPS

KEEPER

GULLY

POINT

SQUARE LEG

EXTRA COVER

MID-OFF

WIDE MID-ON

A DEFENSIVE FIELD SET FOR A PACE BOWLER LATE IN A RUN CHASE

THIRD MAN

FINE LEG

KEEPER

BACKWARD POINT

DEEP SQUARE LEG

DEEP COVER POINT

MID-WICKET

EXTRA COVER

MID-OFF

LONG-ON

SPIN BOWLING EXPLAINED

Monty Panesar has
Brendon McCullum
caught by Paul
Collingwood

ENGLAND
CRICKET

Spin bowling is named after the rapid rotation the bowler attempts to impart on the ball. This spin manifests itself in deviation off the pitch if the ball lands on its seam and grips the surface. This deviation is designed to make it harder for the batter to assess where the ball will arrive and how to play it. It was traditionally called 'break off the pitch', but is now more commonly referred to simply as side or barrel spin (see Figure 1 overleaf).

In addition to break or spin off the pitch, the spin bowler can also try to deceive the batter with over or top spin. This type of spin tends to increase the bounce off the pitch, again assuming the ball lands on the seam as intended (see Figure 2 overleaf).

In reality bowlers will almost always bowl the ball with a combination of side and over spin so that it both turns and bounces, giving two opportunities to deceive the batter. This combination is dictated by the angle of the bowler's wrist at release, which will be covered in more detail later in this section.

In addition to the options of side and over spin, the spinner can also deceive the batter through the air. This involves the batter misreading cues picked up in the flight of the ball and incorrectly assessing where it will land. This can result in poor shot selection, which will increase the chance of the batter being dismissed. This deception has traditionally been called 'flight' or 'loop' but is in fact two different phenomena called drop and curve.

Drop is created by the over spin (again see Figure 2) on the ball which causes it to dip more suddenly than one would expect, often landing further away from the batter than they anticipate.

Curve (or drift) is slightly more complex but is caused by the lateral spin created when the seam position is tilted slightly backwards. Bowlers with a slightly round arm action can often get curve or drift, as

they tend to somewhat undercut the ball as they bowl. Figure 3 shows the rotation around the vertical axis which causes curve.

Drop and curve occur due to a scientific principle called the Magnus effect. Heinrich Magnus, a 19th century German physicist, discovered that a rapidly spinning sphere will curve in the air as a result of its spinning motion, affecting the airflow around one side of the sphere. His discovery was prompted by watching his friends play tennis, and it is tennis which provides the best practical examples of drop and curve. Drop is similar in nature to a top-spin forehand in tennis where the over spin imparted by the racket on the ball at impact causes it to dip severely on its path once over the net. Curve or drift is similar to the side spin imparted on a tennis ball by a sliced serve, which causes it to curve as it travels towards the service court on the other side of the net.

In summary, there are four principal ways that a spin can deceive a batter, and any one of these, or a combination of more than one, can be used to effect a dismissal:

- Side spin/break off the pitch
- Over spin/bounce off the pitch
- Drop/flight through the air
- Curve/drift through the air

The spinner can also use additional variations such as change of pace, angle of delivery, over and round the wicket to try and further deceive the batter.

The primary tactical objective for any spinner should be to draw the batter forward and invite them to drive. This is where the greatest potential for deception lies. Thereafter there are numerous tactical variations a spinner can employ to deceive the batter and effect a dismissal.

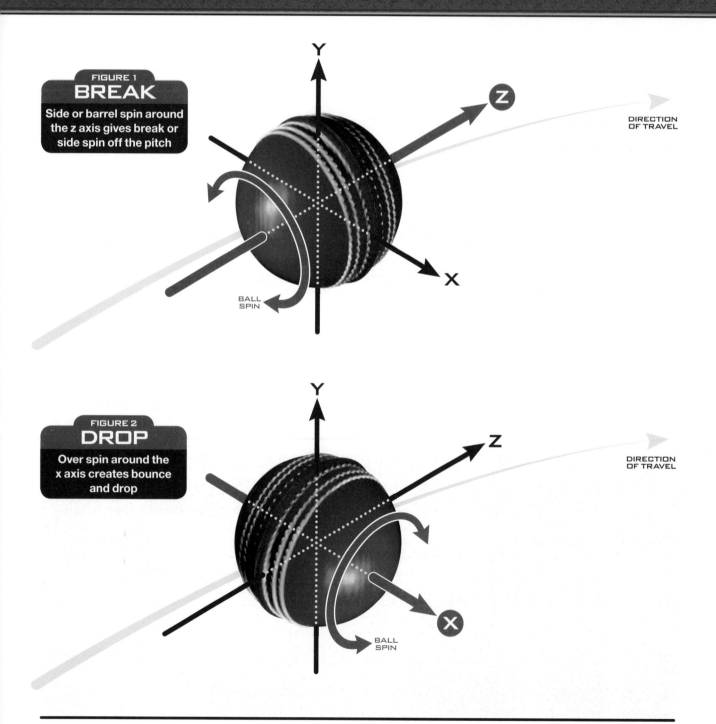

FIGURE 1
BREAK
Side or barrel spin around the z axis gives break or side spin off the pitch

Y

Z

DIRECTION OF TRAVEL

X

BALL SPIN

FIGURE 2
DROP
Over spin around the x axis creates bounce and drop

Y

Z

DIRECTION OF TRAVEL

X

BALL SPIN

ENGLAND
CRICKET

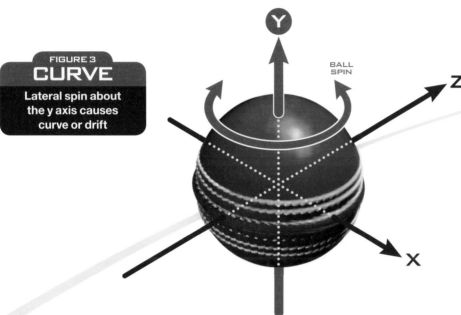

FIGURE 3
CURVE
Lateral spin about
the y axis causes
curve or drift

Y

BALL
SPIN

Z

DIRECTION
OF TRAVEL

X

NB A young spinner who is still not fully grown should not be concerned that they are not yet able to spin the ball greatly. This will tend to come with time as the bowler grows and gets stronger. Every effort should be made, however, to develop the other key characteristics as part of an overall development plan.

Young spin bowlers also need to be protected as they develop. Spin bowling is a difficult art to master and sometimes a young spinner concedes a lot of runs when things do not go to plan. Coaches and captains must learn to persist with young spinners regardless, and allow them to develop and learn in live match situations.

KEY CRITERIA FOR A SUCCESSFUL SPINNER

A spinner's job is to take wickets. To achieve this they must have the ability to influence the behaviour of the ball in the ways described in order to deceive the batter. They must also have the ability to land the ball consistently in an area that creates doubt in the batter's mind and makes it difficult to score runs.

To achieve these desired outcomes, a spin bowler should either possess or be developing the characteristics listed here.

Ability to spin the ball with a vigorous spinning action
Ability to create deception in the ball's flight
A set of effective variations
Control and consistency
Tactical awareness
Physical fitness
Mental strength

These characteristics are greatly aided by:

Good alignment of the bowling action towards the target
A strong and repeatable action
Commitment and a strong work ethic

FINGER SPINNER'S ACTION

There are two types of finger spinner – the right-arm off spinner and the left-arm orthodox spinner. Both attempt to spin the ball using the same technique and an almost identical action, but for obvious reasons the direction of spin is different. The off spinner will normally try to spin the ball from left to right with a clockwise rotation on the ball (as they see it). The left-arm orthodox will try to spin the ball from right to left with an anti-clockwise rotation. The off spinner will tend to bowl over the wicket to the right-hander and round to the left, while the left-armer will tend to bowl round the wicket to the right-hander and over to the left. The modern game is much less prescriptive in these matters, however, with bowlers seeking to use more tactical variations, including bowling a combination of over and round the wicket more often.

The finger spinner's action is similar to that of the pace bowler in some ways, while being different in others. The action still consists of a straight bowling arm rotating vertically around the shoulder joint to impart energy on the ball to propel it. (As has been explained earlier, a 'straight' bowling arm is defined as one which may flex at the elbow to a limit of 15° from straight.) And like pace bowlers, spinners should attempt to bowl with their arm fully extended to prevent the risk of 'throwing', which is deemed an illegal delivery.

The finger spinner's action also differs in many ways from that of the pace bowler, as spin and flight are at a premium rather than pace. Spinners tend to bowl the ball at speeds of around 45–60mph. As a result there are some key differences in the pace and nature of the movement patterns which give the spinner the best chance of being consistently successful. The spinner does, however, go through the same complex sequence of movements as the pace bowler, and it is similarly helpful to break the action down into key phases, as shown over the next three pages.

THE BASIC GRIP
The basic grip is as depicted here (shown for a right-hander but equally applicable to a left-hander):

- Two-fingered grip with thumb playing no active part
- First knuckle joint of the index and middle fingers spread across the seam as widely as possible
- Spinning motion is imparted principally by the index finger
- Index finger dragged along the seam and downwards

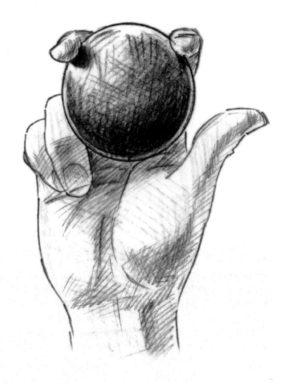

NB It is important to recognise that these are general technical principles and that some bowlers may not adhere to all or even most of these. The integrity of each individual bowling action should always be protected while recognising that the principles mentioned above tend to help develop and improve performance.

Monty Panesar

RUN-UP/APPROACH

GATHER

Usually much shorter than that of the pace bowler (approx 5–10 paces). To encourage alignment of movement towards the target, approach should be relatively straight, with a slight angle (not exceeding 20°) to encourage smooth transition into delivery stride.

- Starting with small steps, approach should be smooth and rhythmical
- Gradual acceleration to a pace which enhances bowling action
- A slight forward lean on the run-up with arms staying close to body
- Head remains steady and upright with eyes fixed on target
- Smooth crossover at transition to side-on delivery stride

This is the transition phase from the approach to the delivery stride. The bowler moves from a front on position on take off through 90 degrees to side on in the pre delivery phase.

- The feet follow a normal stride pattern
- The arms remain close to the body
- Momentum should remain towards target
- Body turns approximately 90 degrees in air
- Head and body remain upright through transition

PRE-DELIVERY

This is when the back foot makes contact with the ground prior to establishing the 'bowling base'. Spinners normally land side-on to the target – this helps to engage the larger muscle groups in the spinning action.

- Back leg remains stable to support the body
- Body remains upright and moving towards target
- Shoulders turn 90° to align with hips
- Hands and arms remain close to body within width of shoulders
- Head remains steady and upright

DELIVERY STRIDE

This is the point at which the front foot lands, creating the solid 'bowling base' that helps propel the ball towards the target. The delivery stride should be long enough to create a strong base but short enough to allow for strong drive over the front leg.

- Front and back foot landing points are generally aligned towards target
- Front leg stabilises and braces prior to commencement of shoulder rotation
- Front arm pushes out towards target to commence shoulder rotation
- Arms and shoulders rotate vertically towards the target
- Head remains steady and as upright as possible

RELEASE

The point at which the bowler lets go of the ball towards the intended target area, with momentum transferring forwards towards the target.

- The ball is released in front of the body, ideally spinning upwards
- Delivery arm ideally just below the vertical
- Body remains as upright as possible on release
- Vertical shoulder rotation towards target over (not round) a braced front leg
- Front arm remains close to body at point of release
- Head remains steady and as upright as possible

FOLLOW-THROUGH

When the ball has been released and momentum has been transferred over the front leg towards target.

- Body continues to move towards target
- Back leg folds up and drives through towards target
- Shoulder rotation continues, completing 180° vertical rotation
- Bowling arm finishes off movement in general across body
- Front arm releases behind body
- Head remains upright and fixed on ball

DIFFERENT DELIVERIES

ENGLAND
CRICKET

England spinners Monty
Panesar and Graeme Swann
prepare to bowl in training

NB To avoid confusion the following explanations
assume the ball is being bowled to a right-handed
batter, unless stated otherwise

OFF-BREAK

The stock delivery of the off-spin bowler,
this ball will generally be bowled over the
wicket from a mid-crease position or
slightly closer to the stumps. It is aimed
outside the right-handed batter's off stump,
inviting the batter to drive or to play a
forward defensive shot. This invites many
forms of dismissal, including bowled,
caught, stumped and LBW. The principles
involved in this delivery would replicate
those of a left-arm spinner bowling to a left-
handed batter over the wicket.

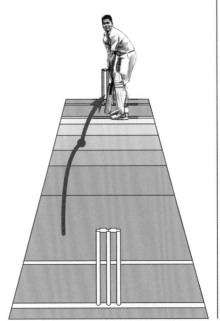

LEFT-ARM OFF-BREAK

The stock delivery of the left-arm (orthodox)
spin bowler, this ball will generally be
bowled round the wicket from a mid-crease
position or slightly wider. It is usually aimed
towards the off stump, or closer to the
middle stump if the wicket is turning sharply,
inviting the batter to drive or to play a
forward defensive shot. This invites many
forms of dismissal, including bowled,
caught, stumped and even LBW if the ball
does not turn. The principles involved in this
delivery would replicate those of an off
spinner bowling to a left-handed batter
round the wicket.

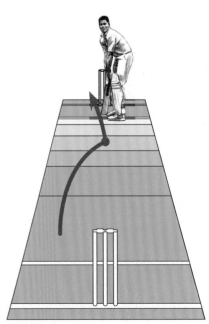

ARM BALL   TOP SPINNER   DOOSRA

This delivery is similar in nature to an out-swing delivery for an off spinner (or an in-swinger for a left-arm spinner), but bowled at a pace just slightly quicker than the stock delivery. The grip is similar to that of an out-swinger but disguised more, with the ball deeper in the hand and the index finger running along the seam (as shown). This tactical variation can be used to deceive the batter in several ways. For an off spinner bowling to a right-hander (or a left-armer bowling to a left-hander), the idea is to either clip or beat the outside edge of the bat. This can result in a catch behind the wicket or a stumping if the batter has left their ground. For a left-arm spinner bowling to a right-hander (or off spinner bowling to a left-hander) the idea is to clip or beat the inside edge of the bat. This can also result in several forms of dismissal, including bowled, LBW or caught close to the wicket.

A top spinner is effectively an over spinner where the ball is bowled with an off spin grip and action but the wrist is turned by 90° so that the seam is facing directly towards the target and the spin becomes complete over spin. The desired outcome of the top spinner is a greater degree of drop and increased bounce off the pitch. This can lead to the batter mistiming an attacking shot and being caught in either the infield or outfield. Alternatively, it can result in the batter being hit high on the bat or the glove playing a defensive shot and being caught close to the wicket.

The term 'Doosra' is Urdu and Hindi for 'other one'. It is effectively the off spinner's or left-armer's googly. It is bowled with an almost identical grip and action to a standard off-break, the only difference being that the palm of the hand is turned by nearly 180° to face the batter. This change in wrist position effectively reverses the direction of spin and can deceive the batter into thinking the ball is turning the other way, with obvious consequences. It is extremely difficult to bowl a Doosra while keeping the bowling arm relatively straight, and good wrist flexibility is required to keep the Doosra legal.

● LEFT-ARM SPINNER
◉ OFF SPINNER

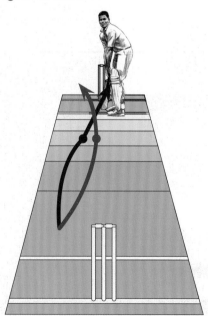

● LEFT-ARM SPINNER
◉ OFF SPINNER

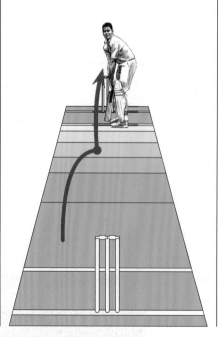

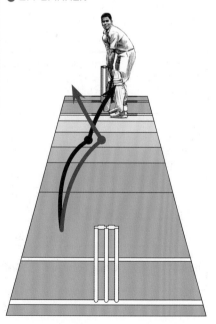

ENGLAND
CRICKET

OTHER VARIATIONS

There are further variations that a spin bowler can also use to deceive the batter. These include subtle changes of pace, varying the angle of delivery on the crease, bowling over and round the wicket, and bowling 'long balls' from behind the crease. It is also important to remember that as the human body is not a perfect machine each delivery will have a degree of natural variation.

HAND AND WRIST POSITION

As alluded to earlier, the position of the wrist is key to the combination of side and over spin on the ball. Different wrist positions will produce different outcomes in terms of turn and bounce. The table below shows the various wrist positions for an off spinner.

HAND AND WRIST POSITIONS FOR FINGER SPINNERS

Wrist position	Type of delivery	Desired outcome
Palm of hand facing batter	Big-turning off-break	Maximum side spin
Palm of hand at 45° to target	Stock ball – part top spin, part side spin	Turn, drop/ bounce and potentially some curve/ drift
Palm of hand at 90° to target	Top spinner	Dip – deceptive length, excessive bounce
Back of hand facing batter	Doosra	Reverses the natural direction of spin
Palm of hand facing upwards	Under cutter	Drift/curve

OFF-BREAK AND DOOSRA
SPOT THE DIFFERENCE

Sri Lankan 'super' spinner Muttiah Muralitharan releases an off-break in practice

The same bowler releases a Doosra during the same session. The key difference is the hand position at point of release

As described in the table, the top image is an off-break with the palm of the hand facing the batter. The lower image is a Doosra with the back of the hand facing the batter, thus reversing the spin.

WRIST SPINNER'S ACTION

Similar to the finger spinners, there are two types of wrist spinner. The right-arm wrist spinner is usually referred to as a leg spinner, although this is in fact just their stock delivery. The left-arm wrist spinner is normally called a left-arm leg spinner or 'Chinaman'. This odd name is believed to derive from the 1930s, when West Indian left-arm spinner Ellis Achong is believed to have been the earliest exponent of the art.

Both 'Leggie' and 'Chinaman' bowlers attempt to spin the ball using the same technique and an almost identical action, but for obvious reasons the direction of spin is different. The leg spinner will normally try to spin the ball from right to left with an anti-clockwise rotation on the ball (as they see it). The left-arm leg spinner will try to spin the ball from left to right with a clockwise rotation on the ball. The leg spinner will tend to bowl over the wicket to the right-hander and round to the left, while the left-hander will tend to bowl over the wicket to both right- and left-handers. But as with finger spinners, the modern game is much less prescriptive in such matters, and wrist bowlers generally seek to use more tactical variations, including bowling over and round the wicket.

Though the wrist spinner's action is similar to that of the finger spinner in most ways, their stock delivery tends to be slightly slower (around 45–55mph compared to 45–60mph), with the nature of the action generally creating more spin, flight, drop and curve than that of the finger spinner.

As a result of this more dynamic movement, leg spin is seen as a more potent attacking weapon than finger spin, and it has undergone a renaissance in the last 10–15 years, principally through the exploits of Shane Warne and Anil Kumble in the test match arena. The flipside to the wonderful art of leg spin, however, is that – like many art forms – it is extremely difficult to master, and accuracy is far more difficult to achieve. As a result some key differences are required in the nature of the movement patterns in order to give leg spinners the best chance of being consistently successful.

Compared with the finger spinner, the leg spinner goes through a similar but slightly more complex sequence of movements, and it is helpful if we break the action down into key phases, as shown on the next three pages.

THE BASIC GRIP

The basic grip is as depicted here (shown for a right-hander but equally applicable to a left-hander):

- Three-fingered grip (also referred to as the 'two up, two down' grip), with thumb playing no active part
- First knuckle joint of index and middle fingers sits across the seam with bent third finger along the seam
- Spinning motion is imparted principally by the third finger
- Third finger drags up and along the seam to initiate rotation

NB It is important to recognise that these are general technical principles and that some bowlers may not adhere to all or even most of these. The integrity of each individual bowling action should always be protected while recognising that the principles mentioned above tend to help develop and improve performance.

ENGLAND CRICKET

Adil Rashid

RUN-UP/APPROACH

Usually much shorter than that of the pace bowler (approx 5–10 paces). To encourage alignment of movement towards the target, approach should be relatively straight, with a slight angle (not exceeding 20°) to encourage smooth transition into delivery stride.

- Starting with small steps, approach should be smooth and rhythmical
- Gradual acceleration to a pace that enhances bowling action
- A slight forward lean on the run-up with arms staying close to body
- Head remains steady and upright with eyes fixed on target
- Smooth crossover at transition to side-on delivery stride

GATHER

This is the transition phase from the approach to the delivery stride. The bowler moves from a front on position on take off through 90 degrees to side on in the pre delivery phase.

- The feet follow a normal stride pattern
- The arms remain close to the body
- Momentum should remain towards target
- Body turns approximately 90 degrees in air
- Head and body remain upright through transition

PRE-DELIVERY

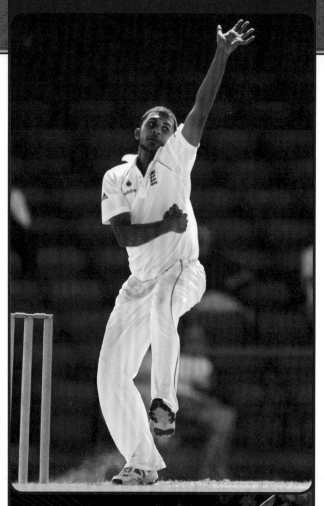

DELIVERY STRIDE

This is when the back foot makes contact with the ground prior to establishing the 'bowling base'. Spinners normally land side-on to the target – this helps to engage the larger muscle groups in the spinning action.

- Back leg remains stable to support the body
- Body remains upright and moving towards target
- Shoulders turn 90° to align with hips
- Hands and arms remain close to body within width of shoulders
- Head remains steady and upright

This is the point at which the front foot lands, creating the solid 'bowling base' which helps propel the ball towards the target. The delivery stride should be as long as is comfortable.

- Front and back foot landing points are generally aligned towards target
- Front leg stabilises and braces prior to commencement of shoulder rotation
- Front arm pushes out towards target to commence shoulder rotation
- Arms and shoulders rotate, somewhere between horizontal and vertical towards target
- Head remains steady and as upright as possible

RELEASE

The point at which the bowler lets go of the ball towards the intended target area, with momentum transferring forwards towards the target.

- The ball is released in front of the body, ideally spinning upwards
- Delivery arm below the vertical (approx 30°)
- Body remains as upright as possible on release
- Shoulder rotation towards target over a braced front leg
- Front arm remains close to body at point of release
- Head remains steady and as upright as possible

FOLLOW-THROUGH

When the ball has been released and momentum has been transferred over the front leg towards the target.

- Body continues to move towards target
- Back leg drives through, allowing hips to rotate around front leg
- Shoulder rotation continues, completing 180° rotation
- Bowling arm finishes off movement in general across body
- Front arm releases behind body
- Head remains upright and fixed on ball

DIFFERENT DELIVERIES

LEG-BREAK

The stock delivery of the wrist spinner, this ball will generally be bowled over the wicket from a mid-crease position. It is usually aimed around the off stump or middle/ middle and leg if the ball is turning sharply. The general aim is to invite the batter to drive or play a forward defensive shot. This invites many forms of dismissal, including bowled, caught, stumped and even LBW if the ball does not turn. The principles involved in this delivery would replicate those of a left-arm leg spinner bowling to a left-handed batter over the wicket.

TOP SPINNER

A top spinner is effectively an over spinner where the ball is bowled with a leg-spin grip and action but the wrist is turned by 90° so that the seam is facing directly towards the target and the spin becomes complete over spin. The desired outcome of the top spinner is a greater degree of drop and increased bounce off the pitch. This can lead to the batter mistiming an attacking shot and being caught in either the infield or outfield. Alternatively, it can result in the batter being hit high on the bat or the glove playing a defensive shot and being caught close to the wicket.

GOOGLY

The opposite of the leg-break. It is bowled with an almost identical grip and action to a standard leg-break, the only difference being that the wrist is turned by almost 180° with the back of the hand facing the batter at release. This change in wrist position effectively reverses the direction of spin and can deceive the batter into thinking the ball is turning the other way, with obvious consequences.

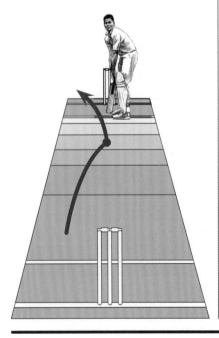

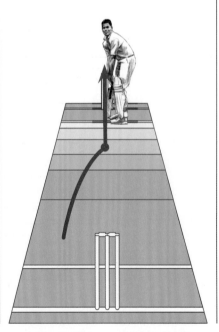

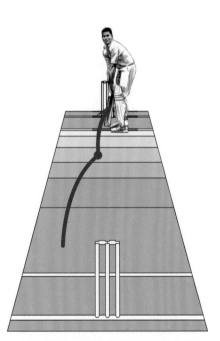

ENGLAND
CRICKET

FLIPPER

The one variation in which a leg spinner uses a different grip. The ball is squeezed between the thumb under the ball and the index and middle fingers on top of the ball. The ball is released with a back-spin motion initiated by flicking the thumb towards the target. Rather than turning away from the bat like a normal leg spinner or into the batter like a googly, the flipper skids on low and fast after pitching. This is designed to catch batters unawares and can result in them being bowled under the bat or LBW.

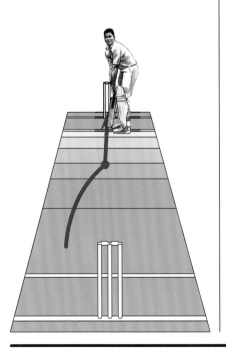

OTHER VARIATIONS

There are further variations that a wrist-spin bowler can also use to deceive the batter. These include subtle changes of pace, varying the angle of delivery on the crease, and bowling over and round the wicket. It is also important to remember that as the human body is not a perfect machine each delivery will have a degree of natural variation.

WRIST POSITION

As with a finger spin bowler, the position of the wrist is key to the combination of side and over spin on the ball. Different wrist positions will produce different outcomes in terms of turn and bounce. The table below shows the various wrist positions for a leg spinner.

WRIST POSITIONS FOR LEG SPINNERS

Wrist position	Type of delivery	Desired outcome
Palm of hand facing batter	Big-turning leg-break	Maximum side spin
Palm of hand at 45° to target	Stock ball – part top spin, part side spin	Turn, drop/bounce and potentially some curve/drift
Palm of hand at 90° to target	Top spinner	Dip – deceptive length, excessive bounce
Palm of hand facing behind bowler	Googly	Reverses the natural direction of spin
Palm of hand facing ground	Flipper	Ball stays low and skids on

SETTING FIELDS FOR SPIN

Cricket has changed dramatically in the past decade in relation to setting fields for spin bowlers. There are now three distinctly different formats of the game, more variations are being used by bowlers, and differing tactics are being employed by both batters and bowlers. This has made the setting of fields much more flexible and the changing of fields far more frequent. Two examples of fields set for spin bowlers are shown here.

STANDARD FIELD FOR A RIGHT-ARM OFF SPINNER IN A ONE-DAY MATCH

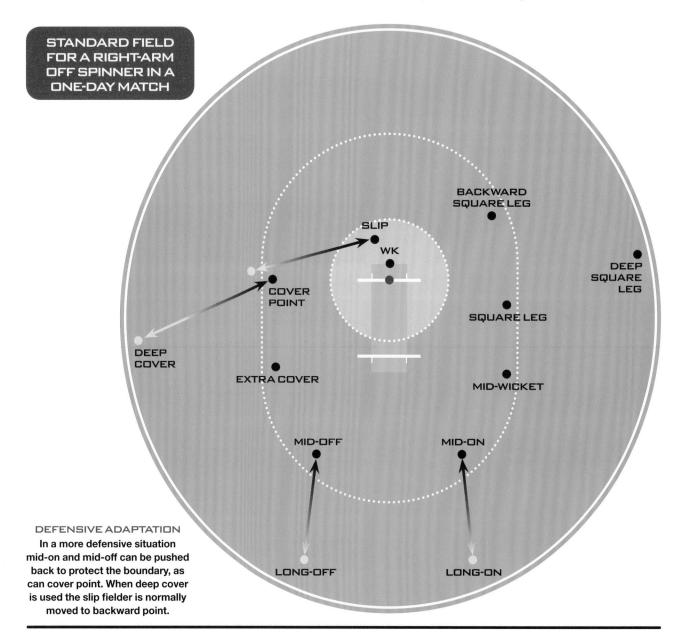

DEFENSIVE ADAPTATION
In a more defensive situation mid-on and mid-off can be pushed back to protect the boundary, as can cover point. When deep cover is used the slip fielder is normally moved to backward point.

ENGLAND
CRICKET

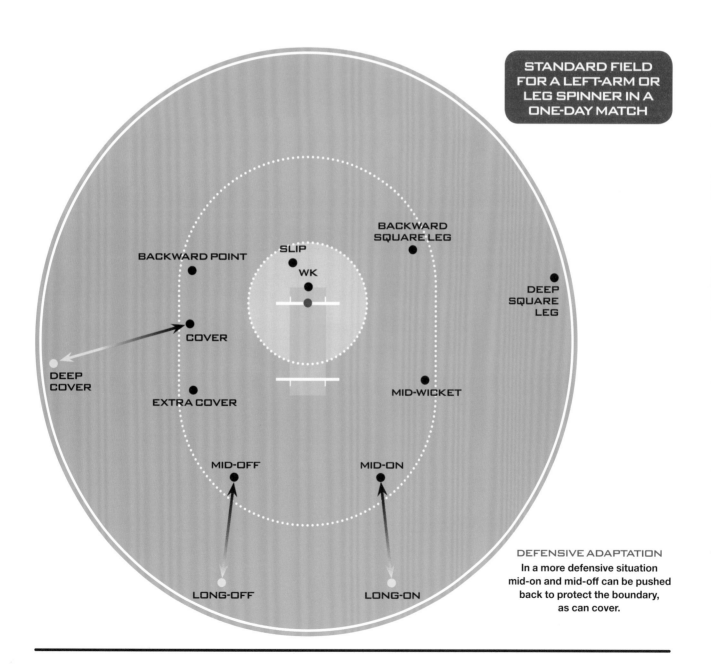

**STANDARD FIELD
FOR A LEFT-ARM OR
LEG SPINNER IN A
ONE-DAY MATCH**

BACKWARD
SQUARE LEG

SLIP

BACKWARD POINT

WK

DEEP
SQUARE
LEG

COVER

DEEP
COVER

EXTRA COVER

MID-WICKET

MID-OFF

MID-ON

DEFENSIVE ADAPTATION
In a more defensive situation
mid-on and mid-off can be pushed
back to protect the boundary,
as can cover.

LONG-OFF

LONG-ON

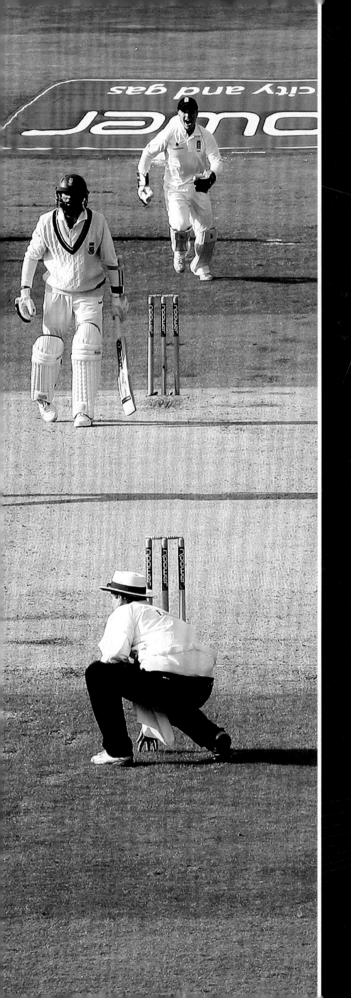

FIELDING

4

INTRODUCTION TO FIELDING

Yorkshire's Anthony McGrath prepares to take a catch at slip off the bowling of Adil Rashid

The fielding team in a standard game of cricket consists of 11 players. This is made up of a bowler, a wicketkeeper and nine fielders. The fielders are strategically placed by the captain, usually in consultation with other key players, to meet the objectives of the fielding team. These objectives are two-fold: to bowl out the batting team by taking all ten wickets, and to concede as few runs as possible in the process.

Fielding has become significantly more important since the advent of limited-overs cricket. Prior to this, it was often seen as a poor relation to batting and bowling. Catching was always seen as being fairly important due to its direct relevance to wicket-taking, but little emphasis was placed on the standard of ground fielding and throwing. The increased need to save runs in limited-overs matches, however, has revolutionised attitudes to fielding. As a result, fielding techniques have improved significantly in the past few decades and the level of improvement continues to accelerate. Developing fielding skills is now seen as a

vital part of any player's training regime, with as much practice time dedicated to it as to batting or bowling.

Fielding has become such an integral part of the modern game that it is often used as a yardstick for performance. If a team has a pack mentality, is energetic in the field and is executing the basic skills well, then it sends a message that the team is on form, together, and well-drilled. It is also the one discipline in the game where players are asked to do hard work largely unnoticed. It is a gauge of players' willingness to put their bodies on the line and make anonymous sacrifices in the name of the team. How well they do this says a great deal about how together and committed a team really is. Even the notion that this sacrifice goes 'largely unnoticed' is now changing, with coaches starting to place objective measures on fielding skills in both training and match situations. This makes a fielder's contribution more measurable and will almost certainly lead to players in the future being judged by some sort of fielding 'average'.

Despite the increase in attention being paid to

fielding by players and coaches alike, the basic principles remain the same. The job of the nine fielders and the wicketkeeper is to support the bowler, help take wickets, and minimise the number of runs scored. Fielders can do this in several ways:

- By catching the ball off the bat to dismiss the batter.
- By stopping the ball to reduce the number of runs scored.
- By throwing the ball at the stumps, or to the wicketkeeper or bowler, to either prevent a run or effect a run-out.

This simplifies the essential functions of a fielder into three simple tasks – catch, stop and throw. The following section will address and put into context the different techniques that fielders use to accomplish these tasks successfully.

It is also important to consider the physical and mental qualities that the best fielders possess. This will help to raise awareness of these desired qualities and can, through good training programmes, help players to acquire and develop these qualities. This in turn will help improve the performance of players on the field.

The tactical placing of fielders by the captain and bowler is crucial if the fielding team is to win the battle between bat and ball. Bowlers will also tend to formulate individual tactical plans to dismiss each batter, so that a variety of tactical battles may be taking place at the same time. The effective placing of fielders combined with successful execution of technique is crucial to the success of any tactical plan. It is therefore important to understand the different fielding areas and positions and the specific tasks that are required for each position in any given situation. Fielders today also need to be multi-positional, as most will be asked to field in more than one type of position through the course of a match.

Dan Housego of Middlesex is congratulated on a run-out

FIELDING ROLES EXPLAINED

Stuart Broad fields on the boundary at Lord's

The type of role a player is asked to carry out in the field tends to be dependent on how far they are fielding from the bat. To help identify the nature of these roles, the field can be roughly separated into three concentric circles. The three areas are populated in general terms by three different types of fielders. These are:

- Close catchers
- Infielders
- Outfielders

CLOSE CATCHERS

These field closest to the bat, either behind or in front of the wicket. They are seen as attacking options that are deployed with the intention of catching the ball from either a defensive or attacking shot. They normally take up a static 'ready' position in anticipation of a catch. The desirable qualities for a close fielder are good hands, co-ordination and agility in order to move and dive around to field and catch balls. Close fielding positions include the slips, gully, silly point, short leg, silly mid-on and silly mid-off. In professional limited-overs matches two 'static' fielders are required in a catching position as a part of fielding restrictions known as a 'power play'. Andrew Flintoff is regarded as one of the world's best slip fielders, mainly due to his 'safe' hands, which ensure he catches the ball when opportunities are presented.

INFIELDERS

These are normally the most athletic and valuable members of the fielding team. This is due to the key area of the field which they patrol. They tend to move in at delivery in a low, cat-like posture, ready to pounce on any opportunities to field or catch the ball. Infielders have the best chance to save runs and create run-outs, as they are in the area of the field that has most traffic – in other words the ball is in this part of the field most often, especially in limited-overs matches where batters are trying to steal runs at every opportunity. Infielders – or ring fielders, as

**ENGLAND
CRICKET**

they are sometimes known – have to regularly demonstrate all of the catch, stop and throw fielding skills at speed and under extreme pressure. As a result speed, agility, power and accuracy of throwing, allied to the ability to dive, catch and slide, are all desirable qualities for the infielder. The premier infielding position is generally accepted to be cover point, the position that sees the most dynamic action. Other infielding positions include mid-wicket, mid-on, mid-off and extra cover. Paul Collingwood is regarded as an expert cover point fielder and one of the world's best.

OUTFIELDERS

These also known as boundary fielders or, in some positions more square of the wicket, as 'sweepers'. Like infielders, outfielders also tend to move in towards the batter at delivery, but more slowly, as they tend to have more time to anticipate the arrival of the ball. The

boundary fielder generally has three principal tasks to carry out. Firstly, to prevent a well-struck ball from going over the boundary and return it to the wicketkeeper or bowler. Secondly, to run in and intercept a less well-struck ball and return it to the keeper or bowler to prevent more runs being taken by the batters. And thirdly, to try and catch any balls 'skied' up into the outfield and thus to dismiss the striking batter. Outfielders, like infielders, should also have speed, ability to dive, a good powerful throw and good catching hands. Outfield positions tend to be the 'deep' variations of the standard infield positions, such as deep cover, deep mid-wicket, long on and long off. Due to the similar nature of the skill set required, good infielders also tend to be effective sweepers and boundary fielders. As a result infielders tend to migrate to the outfield in the latter stages of a limited-overs match when saving boundaries becomes more important than saving singles.

OUTFIELDERS

INFIELDERS

CLOSE
CATCHERS

KEY FIELDING POSITIONS

The diagram on the facing page provides a guide to the somewhat curious names of the many fielding positions and their location on the field. The origin of many of the names is shrouded in the mists of time, and although sense can be made of some, others are less understandable and remain unexplained. Irrespective of the names used, it is important for players to understand where these positions are on the field, and the language used to help modify them. This knowledge will help players understand where they are meant to be when deployed by the captain.

There are around ten basic fielding positions which are employed regularly. Eight of these to all intents and purposes identify with a sector of the field at varying angles to the batter, while the other two refer to close catching positions. These basic positions can then be modified by using the following prefixes:

■ Short or silly – closer to the bat.
■ Deep or long – further from the bat.
■ Fine or square, wide or straight, forward or backward – moves fielder from side to side depending on position on the field.

It is important to understand that these positions are not fixed and should be used as a guide only. Shrewd captains and astute fielders will have the ability to vary their position, depending on various tactical considerations.

The diagram assumes the batter is right-handed. If the batter was left-handed these positions would be reversed mirror-fashion – in other words, the off side of the wicket would change from the left to the right of the diagram and vice versa for the leg side (or 'on side', as it is also called).

Description of the ten basic positions follows.

FINE LEG

Fielding behind square on the leg side close to the boundary. This is one of the important run-saving positions for the pace bowler. The fine leg tends to come into play when a ball is directed down the leg side (often in error) by the bowler and the batter helps the ball on its way to the

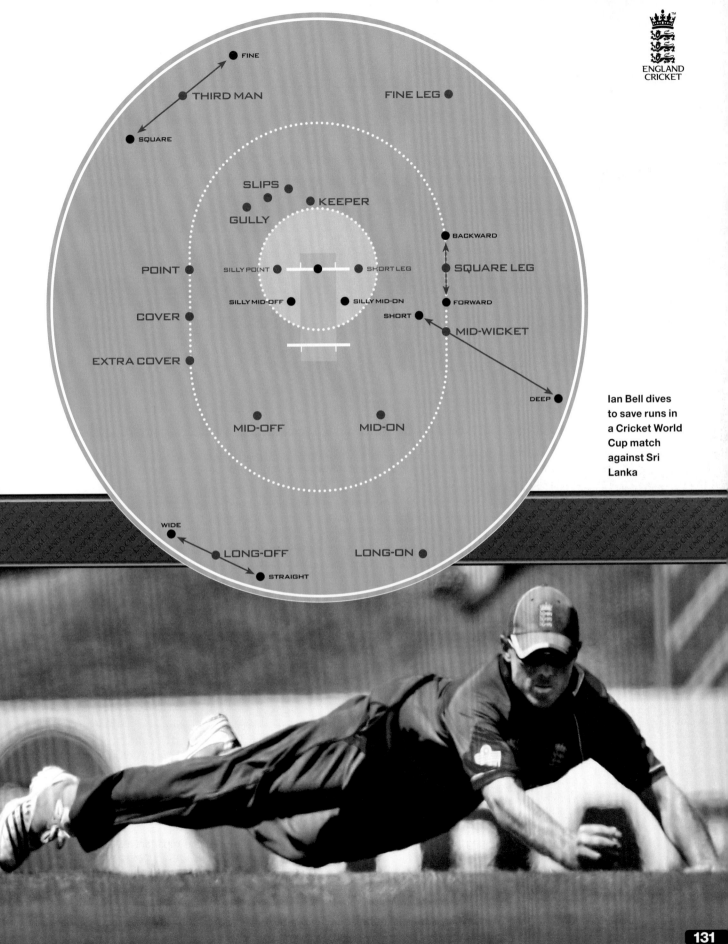

ENGLAND
CRICKET

FINE

THIRD MAN

FINE LEG

SQUARE

SLIPS

KEEPER

GULLY

BACKWARD

POINT SILLY POINT SHORT LEG SQUARE LEG

SILLY MID-OFF SILLY MID-ON FORWARD

COVER SHORT

MID-WICKET

EXTRA COVER

DEEP

MID-OFF MID-ON

WIDE

LONG-OFF LONG-ON

STRAIGHT

Ian Bell dives
to save runs in
a Cricket World
Cup match
against Sri
Lanka

Kevin Pietersen takes a catch at deep square leg against New Zealand

boundary. The fine leg fielder is usually required to intercept and return the ball to the keeper (ground fielding). Occasionally fine leg is required to effect a high catch from a pull shot or top edge. The short fine leg position is used more often for the spinners and is usually required to prevent or 'save' a single run from being scored.

SQUARE LEG

Fields square of the wicket on the leg side, normally close to the square leg umpire. This is a crucial run-saving position and the square leg should be quick and agile to prevent easy runs from being scored in this area. Square leg is often required to take flat, powerfully hit (often diving) catches, which often tend to come square of the wicket. The deep square leg position is more often used for the spin bowlers to protect the boundary, while short square leg, or short leg as it is more commonly known, is a somewhat hazardous close catching position. Short leg is a highly specialist position and will be discussed later in this section.

MID-WICKET

Located in front of square on the leg side of the wicket, this crucial position is arguably second only to cover point as the position where the best fielder should be located. This is due to the 'high traffic' associated with the position, as the ball is often hit, and hit hard, in this area, both on the ground and in

the air. The mid-wicket must be quick and agile with good hands and an accurate throw, to save singles, take catches and create run-outs. Deep mid-wicket is a boundary-saving position that also sees a lot of traffic, particularly near the end of a limited-overs match.

MID-ON

Located in a position straight down the ground from the batter but immediately to the leg or 'on side' of the bowler. Mid-on tends to field balls that are driven hard by the batter towards the boundary. Good hands for catching and fielding and diving stops are often the order of the day in this area. Short or 'silly' mid-on is a strategic catching position for the mis-hit drive, while deep mid-on or long-on is used to protect the straight boundary behind the bowler. This position also tends to see lots of ground fielding and catching action in the later stages of a one-day or Twenty 20 innings.

MID-OFF

This position is very similar to mid-on but is located to the off side of the wicket. Mid-off will also field balls that are driven hard by the batter towards the boundary. Good hands for catching and fielding and the ability to pull off diving stops are crucial. Short or 'silly' mid-off is a strategic catching position for the mis-hit drive, while deep mid-off or long-off is used to protect the straight boundary behind the bowler. This position will almost see as much action as long-on in the later stages of a one-day or Twenty 20 innings.

COVER

Located in front of square on the off side of the wicket, cover or extra cover is an area that sees lots of action. Cover often has to field or catch hard-hit balls on the off side as well as saving runs and creating run-outs. Short cover is a much-used attacking position designed to catch the mis-hit cover drive and tends to be used by both pace and spin bowlers. Deep cover, as the name suggests, is a boundary-protecting position which, again, is much used in limited-overs matches.

POINT

Point, or cover point as it is sometimes confusingly titled, is generally regarded as the most important fielding position, where the best and most athletic fielder is positioned. This is particularly true of the backward point position for pace bowlers. This tends to be the area that the ball travels through most in a one-day or Twenty 20 match. The fielder in this position needs to display the full range of fielding skills, with good hands, speed, agility, throwing power and accuracy all being at a premium. Short point, or silly point as it is also called, is similar to short leg in that it is a highly dangerous and specialised position.

THIRD MAN

Fielding behind square on the off side of the wicket. Like fine leg, this position is often used by the pace bowler to protect the boundary from mis-hits or aggressive cut shots that have evaded the slip cordon. Short third man is a single-saving position more often utilised by the spinners.

SLIP

Placed either individually or in a multiple formation that is referred to as a slip cordon, this is a catching position strategically placed behind the wicket on the off side next to the keeper. The slip fielder, like the keeper, is placed to catch a ball that has glanced the outside edge of the bat. This is the primary form of dismissal achieved by pace bowlers. A safe pair of hands is the primary requirement for this position.

GULLY

Very similar in nature to the slips, this position is located slightly squarer of the wicket and, unlike the slips, there are rarely more than two gullies deployed at once. Again the position is strategically placed to catch a thick edge or a mis-hit drive or cut from the batter. Good hands and agility are highly desirable for this position.

SHORT LEG AND SILLY POINT

In addition to these ten basic positions, there are the two close-catching variations of the square leg and point positions, known as short leg and silly point. As mentioned earlier, these are slightly hazardous positions located close to the bat on the leg and off sides respectively. They are often now referred to as 'bat-pad' catchers due to the nature of the catches they take. They are strategically placed to catch a misjudged defensive shot that can either deflect straight off the bat or off the bat and then the pad. The danger comes in the fielder's proximity to the batter. A hard-hit shot from the batter has the potential to cause serious injury to the fielder, and adequate protection – including helmet, shin pads and abdominal protector – is essential. In the UK these positions are also not permitted in organised junior matches for players aged under 15.

Not Red Nose Day, but Andrew Strauss preparing to take a slip catch against the West Indies

Surrey v Lancashire, County
Championship, 2008

ENGLAND
CRICKET

FIELD PLACEMENT TACTICS

The positioning of the nine available fielders (ie, excluding the bowler and wicketkeeper) is a crucial part of the tactical battle between bat and ball. The overall responsibility for this rests with the captain of the fielding team, but is more often done in partnership with the bowler. The success of these tactics usually depends on how well the field is set in relation to the bowler's tactical plan, allied to the bowler's ability to execute that plan. A well-placed field supporting a sound tactical approach by the bowler gives the fielding team its best chance of dismissing the batter, whereas a poorly set field, even with a good bowling plan, can significantly reduce the fielding team's chances of success.

The art of good field placement is to strike the appropriate balance between attack and defence, and to get the right balance of fielders on either side of the wicket.

ATTACK AND DEFENCE

There is a great variety of factors which must be taken into consideration by the bowler and fielding captain. These can be many and varied, and include:

■ The match situation
■ How long the batter has been at the crease
■ The batter's preferred style and technique
■ The batter's tactical approach
■ The type of bowler
■ The bowler's tactical approach
■ The state of the wicket
■ The condition of the ball

An attacking field positions the fielders in such a way that they are most likely to take a catch. This tends to involve fielders close to the bat, particularly in the slip and gully areas but also at silly point and short leg. The fielding team will usually tend to employ attacking fields when the batter is in a defensive mindset or when the need to be particularly aggressive arises, for example:

■ With the new ball at the start of a match when the ball is hard and at its most dangerous.

Andrew Flintoff bowls to an ultra-attacking field

■ When the batter is new – early in their innings a batter is more likely to be deceived or to play a poor shot.

■ When starting after a break in play, which provides an opportunity to catch the batter cold when resuming their innings.

■ When the batting team is on the defensive, struggling for form, or scoring runs slowly.

■ Using the premier bowlers as an aggressive tactic to try and create a breakthrough.

■ If the overhead or pitch conditions particularly favour the bowlers.

■ When all else has failed and quick wickets are essential if the fielding team is to be successful.

A defensive field is one that is designed to minimise the number of runs scored by the batter. This is achieved by placing fielders in a more defensive formation, principally in the ring and outfield where the batter is most likely to hit the ball. The fielding team will generally employ defensive fields when the batter appears comfortable with the bowling. This tends to happen when the batter has been in for a good period of time and has scored a substantial number of runs. As a result, the most commonly applied tactic is to set a defensive field designed to restrict the flow of runs and encourage the batter to make an error through frustration – for example:

■ When the batting team needs quick runs to increase their chances of winning the game.

■ If a batter is scoring freely and appears in no trouble – stemming the flow of runs may create frustration and force a misjudged or false shot.

■ If the overhead or pitch conditions favour the batter.

■ By using fill-in or non-premier bowlers when resting the strike bowlers, which may require damage-limitation tactics.

■ When trying to keep a particular batter away from the strike to allow the bowler to bowl at the weaker player.

The fielding team will normally set a field that is a combination of attacking and defensive field positions. This gives the fielding team the opportunity to attack the batter with some field placements while being defensive with others. Many spinners bowl with what are referred to as 'in-out' fields, which will attack the batter with close catchers but also defend the boundaries with two or three outfielders. Successful captains tend to have the knack of knowing when to defend, when to go for all-out attack and, more often than not, when to do a combination of both.

OFF- AND LEG-SIDE FIELDS

When striking a balance between attack and defence the fielding side must also try to create a balance with the appropriate number of fielders on either side of the wicket. Due to the odd number of fielders to be placed (nine), the balance of fielders must inevitably favour one side of the wicket, and this tends to be the off side. This is because most bowlers, especially pace bowlers, try to bowl a line on or just outside off stump. This requires more fielders to be on the off side of the wicket as the ball is more likely to be hit there.

A common field for a pace bowler at the start of a match would feature six fielders on the off side, including two or three close catchers, and three

ENGLAND
CRICKET

fielders on the leg side, usually including one on the fine leg boundary. This is known in cricketing terms as a 6:3 field. This is a reference to the ratio of fielders on either side of the wicket, with the off side stated first. In some exceptional cases attacking fields may become 7:2 or even 8:1 in favour of off-side fielders, usually due to the number of slips and gullies employed. The other most common field, however, tends to be a more balanced 5:4 off-side field. On some occasions bowlers, particularly right-arm off spinners, may choose to bowl a straighter or more leg-side line. In this case the field tends to become a 4:5 leg-side field. This reflects the fact that the ball is more likely to be hit on the leg side. It is very rare for there to be more than six fielders on the leg side as the laws state that no more than two fielders are allowed behind square on the leg side of the wicket. There is also a playing condition that applies in limited-overs matches stating that no more than five fielders are allowed on the leg side.

There are several other fielding restrictions that come into play during limited-overs matches, including no more than five fielders outside the 30-yard fielding circle. The concept of 'power plays' now also applies to both 50- and 20-over matches at professional level. This restriction allows fewer fielders outside the circle and also insists on close catchers during certain portions of the innings. These artificial playing conditions are designed to make the game more entertaining and as a result they also provide challenges for the captain and bowler when setting fields.

Middlesex's off-side fielders move to intercept the ball in the Twenty 20 Cup Final of 2008

FIELDING QUALITIES

Steven Crook of Northants shows agility in taking a diving catch during a Twenty 20 match

The standard of fielding has improved significantly in recent times. Good execution of the traditional skills of catching, ground fielding, chasing and throwing are still fundamental to successful fielding. However, the way in which some of these skills are executed has changed and evolved greatly. This has come about from the increased premium placed on the saving of runs, and also the increased prevalence of limited-overs matches. The recent rise of Twenty 20 cricket has only served to magnify the focus on run-saving. Fielders have adopted the mantra that 'every run is a prisoner', and have to be willing to put their bodies on the line to back this up. As a result the qualities required to become a top-class fielder have become more clearly defined.

The technical skills required to be a good fielder are many and varied, with different positions placing a premium on different skills. But in addition to technical expertise in any specialised area, there are also many generic tactical, mental and physical qualities that are relevant to any position on the field. The following qualities, when developed, can help players to fulfil their potential.

SPEED
The ability to move quickly towards the ball, whether to intercept or chase. This will allow the fielder to get to the

ENGLAND
CRICKET

ball and return it more quickly and thereby help prevent additional runs being scored. The ability to think quickly and make good decisions is also important.

CONCENTRATION

A fielder requires the ability to focus on the critical moments during a match. This state of readiness allows the fielder to block out all distractions and pick up the critical cues that will allow successful execution of the necessary fielding skill.

AGILITY

The ability to change direction quickly and efficiently. This requires a combination of co-ordination, speed, power and balance. An agile fielder has the ability to make simple, smooth and quick body movements that allow them to move to the ball more efficiently.

CO-ORDINATION

The ability to make key parts of the body work together to carry out the required fielding skills. Hand/eye co-ordination would be an obvious example, especially when related to skills like catching.

POWER

The requirement for powerful movements and a powerful throwing arm goes without saying for an all-round fielder.

DURABILITY

Fielders should be able to withstand the stresses of constant diving, throwing and catching. This can take its toll on the body and it is important to be physically robust. It is also helpful to be mentally durable and able to stand up to the emotional pressures created by the business end of the game. The ability to be mentally durable and to bounce back from dropped catches is also highly beneficial. Everyone drops a catch at some stage – the trick is to not allow it to affect your chances of catching the next one.

SIMPLICITY

Good fielding is not a complicated craft. The best fielders tend to have a very simple, straightforward technique and the ability to simplify their thought processes in terms of the options available.

HARD WORK/SELF-SACRIFICE

Getting good at fielding and the fundamental skills that are involved requires hard work. Those who want to excel at fielding must be prepared to put in the hard yards on the training pitch. Good fielders must be

hungry and looking for work and be keen for the ball to come to them. They must also be prepared to sacrifice this time and energy in the best interests of the team and not necessarily themselves.

POSITIVE BODY LANGUAGE

The best fielders have an 'aura' or 'presence' which says to everyone that they mean business and are going to be tough to get the ball past. This is often transmitted through body language and demeanour.

Ed Joyce shows speed taking a running catch for Middlesex during a Twenty 20 match

CLOSE CATCHING

O ne of the best-known sayings in cricket is 'catches win matches'. This shows that the importance of catching cannot be underestimated. Irrespective of how good the bowlers may be and how many other ways there are to dismiss a batter, catches will need to be taken at some stage during the innings. A speculative diving catch can often be the catalyst for a winning performance, whereas a simple catch dropped can often be the demoralising moment that leads to a defeat. If a team is to be successful on a regular basis then the fielders must be able to hold their catches.

There are two basic types of catch – the close catch and the high catch, with the 'skim' or flat catch and diving catch being slight variations of these. The modern game demands that fielders must be multi-positional, so it is important that fielders practise all three types of catch. Fielders who specialise in certain positions will rightly practise the type of catch they are most likely to receive, but it is also important to practise for all eventualities.

CLOSE CATCHING
The majority of catches are taken in attacking positions close to the bat, particularly in the slips or gully. Other areas where close catches are taken

ENGLAND CRICKET

Monty Panesar bowls in New Zealand with close catchers around the bat

include leg slip, leg gully, silly mid-on, silly mid-off, silly point and short leg. The qualities that are most crucial in the close-catching positions tend to be concentration and co-ordination. The catches in each of these positions will come at varying heights, speeds and angles but the technical principles involved in successfully executing close catches remain consistent.

The traditional catching method, with fingers pointing downwards, usually applies to catches below chest height. When the ball is caught above chest height the 'reverse' method is normally used, with the fingers pointing upwards.

KEY POINTS

STANCE

- Ensure optimal distance from batter to achieve comfortable catch
- Feet slightly wider than shoulder width apart
- Weight evenly spread, slightly forward
- Knees flexed, hands together
- Fingers pointing downwards
- Head steady, eyes level

RECEPTION

- Watch ball all the way into hands
- Allow ball to 'arrive' into hands
- Hands or hand give with the ball

KEY POINTS

BOTH TECHNIQUES

- Fielder moving in with intent at delivery
- Low balanced position
- Head steady, eyes level
- Assessing the flight of the ball
- Moves quickly to position under the ball
- Keeps head as steady as possible, eyes fixed on ball
- Creates 'base' underneath ball
- Prepare hands above eye level
- Knees flexed, hands relaxed

TRADITIONAL TECHNIQUE

- Fingers spread and pointing forwards and slightly upwards
- Little fingers touching to present large catching area to ball
- Catch should be made at or just below eye level
- Catch completed with 'give' to chest

REVERSE TECHNIQUE

- Fingers pointing upwards and backwards
- Thumbs together or crossed to present large catching area to ball
- Catch should be made above eye level
- Catch completed with 'give' to side of head into shoulder

Andrew Strauss in position in Sri Lanka to take a catch using the traditional method

ENGLAND CRICKET

FIELDING TECHNIQUES

HIGH CATCHING

Fielders positioned in the 'deep' or outfield close to the boundary – positions such as long-off, long-on, deep cover, deep mid-wicket and deep square leg – are those most likely to have to take a high catch. The qualities most needed when taking a high catch are co-ordination, concentration, speed and agility.

Catches in these positions can often come at varying heights and trajectories. On most occasions the fielder will be able to choose whether or not to take the catch using the 'traditional' method in front of the body with fingers pointing forward. The alternative 'reverse' method is taken closer to the shoulder with fingers pointing backwards. In some cases one or other of these methods will be the more obvious one to use. For example, when having to move forward quickly to take a high catch that arrives low-down near the ground, the traditional method is usually the only option; conversely, when running backwards and taking a catch which arrives above shoulder height the reverse method is normally the only option.

TRADITIONAL TECHNIQUE	REVERSE TECHNIQUE

FIELDING TECHNIQUES

FLAT AND OTHER CATCHES

Fielders who are positioned in the infield around 15–25yds from the bat are often called upon to make flat or 'skim' catches. This type of catch is made to a ball that has been struck firmly by the batter. As a result the ball often travels in a 'flat' trajectory towards the fielder. When the ball is struck firmly but not straight at the fielder, an attempt to dive and catch the ball can often be made in order to pull off a spectacular catch. Close and high catches can also produce a dive from the fielder but this is more common in the infield. Positions such as cover, extra cover, mid-off, mid-on, mid-wicket and square leg are the ones most likely to be offered a flat catch.

The desirable qualities for this type of catch are concentration, speed, power and agility. The flat catch comes at varying heights and speeds and the traditional fingers-pointing-downwards method usually applies to catches below chest height. When the ball is caught above chest height the reverse method, with the fingers pointing upwards, is more effective.

Kevin Pietersen takes a flat catch using
the reverse method during a one-day
international against South Africa

Samit Patel
dives for a catch
in training

ENGLAND
CRICKET

KEY POINTS

FLAT CATCH

- Fielder moving in with intent at delivery
- Low, balanced position
- Fielder should set into a 'goalkeeper' ready position as batter hits ball
- Head steady, eyes fixed on ball
- Solid base should be created to receive ball
- Fingers pointing downwards with hands together (below chest height) or fingers pointing upwards with thumbs together (above chest height)

DIVING CATCH

- Fielder moving in with intent at delivery
- Low, balanced position
- Fielder should set into a 'goalkeeper' ready position as batter hits ball
- Head steady, eyes fixed on ball
- Dive low with head towards ball
- Go with two hands if possible, one if not possible
- Keep eyes fixed on ball
- Attempt to land on chest or shoulder (not elbows) to break fall

GROUND FIELDING

Paul Collingwood fields the ball off his own bowling

The ability to field well is now a crucial part of the cricketer's game. As stated earlier, the quality of fielding is undoubtedly the area of the game where skills have improved most in recent years. Limited-overs cricket has been the catalyst for this and cricket now demands that every run possible is prevented by the fielding team. Ground fielding in particular has seen the most obvious improvements, with fielders becoming more athletic – chasing and diving to intercept and retrieve balls in an attempt to reduce the number of runs scored. The greatly increased number of run-outs in limited-overs matches is evidence of the improvements in ground fielding and throwing accuracy.

Ground fielding can be divided into three specific areas:

■ Attacking interceptions
■ Defensive interceptions
■ Chasing and retrieving

ATTACKING INTERCEPTIONS
There are two types of attacking interception: the one-handed and the two-handed. These are generally used in specific situations which will be explained below, along with the key points involved in the execution of this skill.

THE ONE-HANDED INTERCEPTION

This is normally used when the ball is relatively slow-moving and within ten yards of the stumps. It is seen most often when the batters are attempting to 'steal' a single from a defensive push or deflection off the pads. The fielder then attacks the ball to pick it up one-handed and throw underarm at the stumps in an attempt to run the batter out.

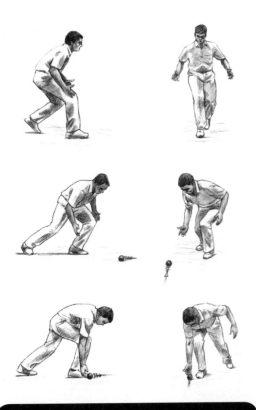

THE TWO-HANDED INTERCEPTION

This skill is normally used either in the infield or the outfield to catch a well-struck ball, but one that the fielder still has the opportunity to move towards and attack. It is demonstrated most often when a batter is attempting to score a run from a ball hit into the infield or attempting a second run from a ball hit into the outfield. The fielder then attempts to pick up one-handed and throw overarm back to the stumps to try and run the batter out.

KEY POINTS

- Fielder moving in with intent at delivery
- Low, balanced position
- Weight on the balls of the feet
- Assess the line, moving quickly towards the ball
- Ball should be picked up outside the throwing foot (right foot for right-hander and vice versa)
- Fingers pointing downwards, watching ball into hand
- Low body position maintained, eyes move to assess target
- Minimal backswing with throwing arm to save time
- Follow through with throwing arm and body moving towards target

KEY POINTS

- Moving in at delivery in a low, balanced position
- Weight on the balls of the feet
- Assess the line, moving quickly towards ball
- Approach slightly to the non-throwing side of ball (left side for right-hander and vice versa)
- Leading hip and non-throwing shoulder turn slightly towards the ball prior to pick-up, giving 45° body angle at pick-up
- Watching the ball, with throwing foot (right foot for right-hander and vice versa) placed behind the ball prior to pick-up
- Non-throwing foot trails behind, allowing balance to be maintained
- Low body position, bending from knees at pick-up
- Eyes watch ball into both hands, fingers pointing downwards
- Eyes move to assess target
- Trailing leg moves through towards target to create a wide throwing base and strong sideways throwing position

DEFENSIVE INTERCEPTIONS

There are also two types of defensive interception: the 'barrier' method, typified by the traditional long barrier, and the diving interception for more desperate situations.

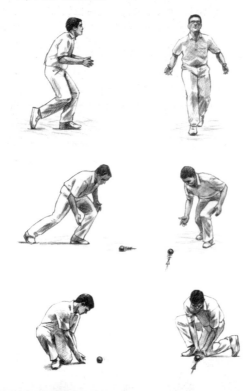

Ian Bell and Andrew Strauss combine to stop a single

This tends to be used in the infield when the ball is struck firmly and directly at the fielder. In this situation the fielder will generally attempt to stop the ball with their hands but will try to use some part of the body as a second line of defence. More often then not this will be the torso or legs. The long barrier is occasionally used in the infield, but more often in the outfield when the ball has been struck hard enough that the primary aim is to prevent the ball from passing the fielder to the boundary.

KEY POINTS

- Moving in at delivery in a low, balanced position
- Weight on the balls of the feet
- Assess the line of the ball, moving quickly into anticipated line
- Leading hip and non-throwing shoulder turn slightly towards the ball prior to pick-up
- Long barrier established at 90° to path of the ball, kneeling on non-throwing knee (left knee for right-hander and vice versa)
- Head over ball at pick-up, fingers downwards, hands together
- Eyes move to assess target
- Fielder rises, standing up on throwing foot
- Non-throwing foot moves towards target to create a wide base and strong sideways throwing position

Used when the ball would normally have been hit beyond the reach of the fielder when in a standing position. The dive becomes necessary when the ball has been struck at such a pace that the fielder cannot move to intercept it in a standing position.

KEY POINTS

- Moving in at delivery in a low, balanced position
- Weight on the balls of the feet
- Assess the line of the ball, moving head and hands towards anticipated line
- Dive from a position as low to the ground as possible
- Watch ball into hands if possible
- Attempt to place hand behind the ball and leave it there as a barrier

ENGLAND CRICKET

Katherine Brunt dives to stop the ball off her own bowling

CHASING AND RETRIEVING

This technique is used when the ball is hit past or over the infield. The fielder needs to turn and chase the ball to prevent it from reaching the boundary and then return it to the wicket as quickly as possible to minimise run-scoring. There are four types of retrieve – short, long, sliding and relay. The first two refer to the distance the ball is chased. The technique for

both is very similar, with one subtle variation for the longer chase. The sliding retrieve has become increasingly popular in the last decade as it is perceived to help the fielder pick up and position for the return throw more quickly. The relay retrieve has also become popular recently and employs two fielders who work together to retrieve and return the ball.

SHORT RETRIEVE (APPROX 5–15YDS)

LONG RETRIEVE (BOUNDARY THROW)

Similar to short retrieve except the pick-up often takes place outside the non-throwing foot or even between the feet. This variation is because the fielder may turn and take a 'crow hop' crossover step back towards target. This creates a stronger base and the forward momentum required for a longer throw.

CROW HOP VARIATION

Paul Collingwood releases a long throw during a practice session

KEY POINTS

- Moving in at delivery in a low, balanced position
- Weight on the balls of the feet
- Fielder turns quickly to give chase, facing the ball
- Assess the line of ball, running slightly to the non-throwing side (left side for a right-hander and vice versa)
- Fielder decelerates if necessary and slightly over-runs the ball
- Pick up in low, balanced position, bending at knees
- Ball picked up on outside of throwing foot (right foot for a right-hander and vice versa)
- Eyes remain on ball, pick up with fingers downwards and hand past the ball, palm facing back towards target
- Turn back towards target using non-throwing arm for aim
- Non-throwing foot moves toward target to create a wide base and strong sideways throwing position

SLIDING RETRIEVE

The sliding retrieve is again similar in most ways to the other retrieves, except that the fielder will over-run the ball by sliding past it on the throwing side (right-hand side for right-hander and vice versa).

KEY POINTS

- Slide starts when fielder is almost level with ball
- Fielder slides level with ball to achieve pick-up
- Throwing foot leads slide (right foot for right-hander), non-throwing foot bends and folds underneath leading leg, forming a figure '4' shape (similar to a sliding tackle in football)
- Fielder picks up ball as turn begins back towards play
- Throwing foot used as brake and to stand up
- Non-throwing leg moves back towards target in flowing movement to create a strong base

RELAY RETRIEVE (NEAR BOUNDARY)

This technique tends to be used very close to the boundary and allows the lead fielder to concentrate on saving the boundary and then feed the ball a short distance to a second fielder (normally no more then ten yards away) who returns it by a long throw to the wicket. The rationale behind this method is the perception that it can save time when well-executed.

Kevin Pietersen uses a sliding
retrieve to prevent a boundary
during a one-day international

ENGLAND
CRICKET

THROWING

Andrew Strauss prepares to throw on the run

Good throwing, along with the diving stop or catch, is the most dynamic area of fielding. A good throw is always appreciated by team-mates and spectators alike, as the outcome is obvious to the eye. Watching a powerfully thrown ball knock the stumps out of the ground to achieve a run-out is one of greatest sights in cricket. Similarly, the sight of a ball thrown from 70yds finding its way directly into the keeper's gloves is a joy to behold, and the running-out of a batter by a dynamic pick-up and throw can often be a game-changing moment. It is therefore essential for a top-class fielder to throw well. The key elements of any successful throw are simple:

■ Power – which allows the ball to reach its target as quickly as possible.
■ Accuracy – which ensures that the ball goes straight to its target, whether this is the stumps or the wicketkeeper.

Different types of throws tend to be used in different situations to achieve the desired outcome. The preferred outcome for the fielding side is a run-out, but it may also be a quick and accurate throw which prevents an extra run being taken. The three main types of throw are:

■ The underarm throw.
■ The overarm throw (short and long).
■ The throw on the run.

**Paul Collingwood
throws underarm during
a practice session**

ENGLAND
CRICKET

THE UNDERARM THROW

This is normally used as an extension of the one-handed interception. This is used when the ball is relatively slow-moving and within about ten yards of the stumps. It tends to be seen when the batters are attempting to 'steal' a single from a defensive push or a deflection off the pads. The fielder then attacks the ball to pick it up one-handed and throw underarm at the stumps in an attempt to run the batter out.

KEY POINTS

- Moving towards the ball in a low, balanced position
- Fingers pointing downwards, watching ball into hand
- Low body position maintained, eyes move to assess target
- Minimal backswing with throwing arm to save time
- Follow through with throwing arm and body moving towards target

THE OVERARM THROW

This is the most powerful of all the throws. The shorter throw is normally used in the infield when trying to prevent a single or second run being taken, and the longer throw is used in the outfield closer to the boundary. The desired outcomes of power and accuracy are produced by adhering as closely as possible to the correct technical model. This model is also important to help maintain a safe throwing technique, as the stresses on the shoulder are high during the overarm throw. These stresses greatly increase the chance of injuries occurring if the throwing technique is poor.

Kevin Pietersen creates a powerful base from which to throw during practice

KEY POINTS

- Ideally ball should be held across seam with thumb underneath (there is not always time to amend the position of the seam)

- Eyes move to and assess target

- Back foot should be 90° to target, long straight stride establishes a strong base to throw from

- Throwing arm drawn back straight and wrist cocked (hand often travels further back for the long, more powerful throw)

- Hips and shoulders begin to rotate towards target, generating power moving upwards through the body

- Non-throwing arm pulls in quickly as upper body uncoils, propelling throwing arm towards target

- At point of release elbow should remain level or slightly above shoulder height to maintain a safe throwing technique

- Ball should be released from a low, balanced position with bent front leg

- Fingers and wrist remain behind ball for as long as possible to point of release

- Upper body completes 180° rotation, trailing leg and hip follow to 90°

ENGLAND
CRICKET

THE THROW ON THE RUN

This is normally used for throws over a shorter distance in the infield when the fielder has had to move sideways to intercept the ball. As time is precious when attempting a run-out, there may be no time to stabilise the body and create a solid base to throw from. As a result of this, the throw may be slightly less powerful, but over a shorter distance this may be less important in terms of saving time.

**Ian Bell throws
at the stumps
on the run**

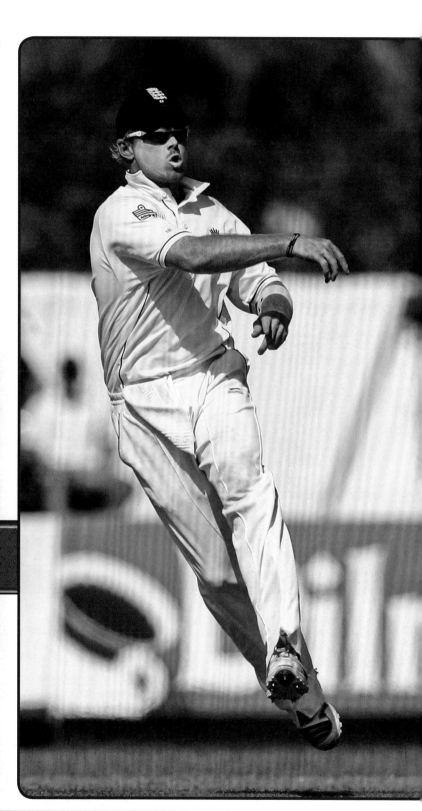

KEY POINTS

- ■ Moving towards the line of the ball in a low, balanced position
- ■ Fingers pointing downwards, watching ball into the hand
- ■ Low body position maintained, eyes move to assess target
- ■ Body rises and throw is executed off back foot without establishing base
- ■ Upper body disassociates with energy from throwing arm propelled towards target, while lower half continues sideways movement
- ■ Throwing arm may drop slightly below shoulder level due to time-saving nature of this throw

WICKETKEEPING TECHNIQUES

INTRODUCTION AND EQUIPMENT

James Foster demolishes the stumps while attempting to run out David Sales of Northamptonshire

The wicketkeeper is a crucial member of every cricket team and the focal point of the fielding unit. The duties of the keeper are so many and varied that it makes the position unique in terms of both involvement in the action and ability to influence the game. As a result the best keepers are worth their weight in gold. The skills and mindset required by a successful keeper are also sufficiently distinctive that the position often attracts a similarly distinctive type of individual – keepers often pride themselves on being *different*.

The wicketkeeper is positioned behind the stumps at the batter's end of the wicket and is the only

member of the fielding side who is allowed to wear gloves to help them catch the ball. The gloves are required because of the volume of catches that the keeper has to take and the high speeds at which the ball is travelling. The major function of a keeper is to stop, and ideally catch, the deliveries that pass the batter. This is to prevent runs being scored. The keeper's positioning will depend on the pace of the bowler. The keeper will 'stand up' just behind the stumps for the slower bowlers and will 'stand back' a good distance from the stumps for the quicker bowlers. The rationale on how far a keeper stands behind the stumps is normally linked to where they are best able to catch the ball comfortably at around waist height.

The keeper also has the ability to dismiss the batter in a number of ways, as outlined below.

CATCH

The most common form of dismissal by the keeper is the catch behind the wicket. This occurs when the keeper catches a ball that has glanced off the edge of the bat and carried on to him without bouncing. Sometimes the keeper is also required to catch a ball that is 'skied' up in the air without travelling any great distance from the batter.

STUMPED

This involves the keeper catching the ball and removing the bails from the stumps when a batter has left their crease in the process of playing a shot. This can only be achieved when the keeper is standing up close to the wicket, mainly to spinners and medium-pacers. The keeper then appeals to the square-leg umpire to adjudge whether the batter had any part of his body or equipment behind the front crease line. If not, then they are given out 'stumped'.

RUN-OUT

This occurs when the ball is returned to the keeper while a batter is attempting a run. It is the keeper's responsibility to move to a position beside or behind the stumps that will allow them to remove the bails as quickly as possible if there is a chance of a run-out. Similar to a stumping, if the batter has no part of their body or equipment grounded behind the front crease line they are adjudged run-out. The keeper also has the opportunity to run a batter out by chasing and fielding the ball and then throwing down the stumps before the batter manages to make their ground. This tells us that keepers must also be able to throw the ball well.

LBW

Although the keeper has no direct involvement in the play leading up to a leg-before-wicket decision, their position directly behind the batter makes them well placed to judge whether or not the ball could have potentially hit the wicket. The keeper's appeal in support of the bowler is an important part of the process, and a confident appeal by the keeper is usually crucial if the appeal is to be successful.

If a keeper is to be successful in helping dismiss batters, the one thing they have to be able to do above all else is catch the ball. In addition to having good hands, a keeper must therefore possess good foot movement, to get them in position to make catches. Developing an effective technique with sound basics will greatly aid the keeper in achieving this primary function. It is important for the keeper to be technically competent both standing up and standing back if they are to perform consistently well.

In order to do this the keeper must possess the correct equipment. Shown below are the crucial pieces of kit for a keeper. Wicketkeepers under the age of 18 are required by ECB Guidelines to wear a helmet when standing up to the wicket.

PADS

HELMET

BOX

GLOVES

STANDING UP

Matt Prior stands up to the wicket as M.S. Dhoni bats in a match between England and India

Standing up to the wicket is said to be the greatest challenge for the wicketkeeper and it is generally accepted that this is where the real art of wicketkeeping lies. The obvious increase in the level of challenge comes from the keeper being positioned closer to the stumps and having less time to assess the line and bounce of the ball. In addition to this the batter is also partially in his line of sight and is wielding his bat in the general direction of the keeper. Therefore courage is also a desirable quality for a keeper standing close to the wicket.

Standing up to the spin bowlers on a dry, turning wicket also provides a formidable challenge to the keeper, with the ball breaking sharply off the pitch and bouncing inconsistently, adding to the degree of difficulty. Many keepers will wear a helmet when standing up to the spinners on a wearing pitch, as the chances of being struck by a ball are dramatically increased. The keeper who can keep a tidy wicket and take all the catches that come their way in these circumstances is a valuable asset to any team.

The best keepers tend to combine key physical and mental attributes allied to a sound technique.

STANCE

- Crouched slightly to the offside of the batter
- Eyes level with clear sight of ball
- Body and hands must remain behind the stumps
- Weight on the balls of the feet
- Relaxed, comfortable position

TAKING THE BALL

- Head and body behind the ball
- Body rises with the bounce of the ball
- For normal take, fingers point downwards
- For high-bouncing take, upper body rotates to take ball to side of the body
- Leg withdraws back and to the side to accommodate bounce

OFF-AND LEG-SIDE TAKE

- Feet and body move to place head in line with ball
- Movement should be smooth to keep head steady
- Hands remain low to rise with ball
- Hands together and give with ball

STUMPING

- When take is completed, body weight transfers towards stumps
- Hands move quickly to break the wicket

STANDING BACK

Geraint Jones prepares to catch Australia's Damien Martyn

Standing back also presents challenges for the wicketkeeper. The extra pace and bounce require the keeper to be extremely athletic. The additional distance the keeper stands back from the wicket gives the ball the potential to deviate much more than when standing up. Therefore the keeper must be prepared to move quickly to take the ball. There is also a greater necessity to dive and catch deflected edges on both sides of the wicket. As a result, keepers need to be comfortable diving either way.

The keeper standing back will tend to move into their stance later than when standing up. They will also tend to crouch less when standing back, to avoid getting 'too set' and stuck in a static position, as this can hinder their ability to get their feet moving quickly. Fast feet are crucial for standing back, as quick movement towards the ball is crucial for the keeper to make consistent catches.

STANCE

- Slightly crouched but less pronounced than when standing up
- Positioned to off side to get clear sight of ball
- Positioned far enough back to take ball at comfortable height

TAKING THE BALL

- Move quickly into position behind ball
- Relax, hands give with ball
- Fingers downwards for waist-high take or below
- Fingers upwards for chest-high take or above
- Keeper may choose to take ball below the eyes or on the inside hip depending on personal preference

OFF-AND LEG-SIDE TAKE

- Feet and body move across to place head in line with ball
- Movement should be smooth to keep head steady
- Hands stay low, rising with bounce of the ball
- Hands together and give with the ball

DIVING TAKE

- Dive low with head towards ball
- Go with two hands if possible, one if not possible and extra stretch is required
- Keep eyes fixed on ball
- Take ball as late as possible
- Attempt to roll on to shoulder on landing to prevent elbows jarring

WICKETKEEPING QUALITIES

James Foster of Essex shows great speed and agility in stumping Darren Stevens of Kent

The demands placed on wicketkeepers have increased significantly in recent times. As with most other areas of the game, limited-overs cricket has changed the face of wicketkeeping.

The keeper has always been the 'piper' for the fielding unit, setting the tone for the tempo of the fielding effort while doing their own job efficiently behind the stumps. The modern game, however, demands that the keeper does even more than in the past. Almost without exception, a keeper now also needs to be a recognised batter, the specialist keeper having been sacrificed in exchange for a keeper/batter, thus allowing teams to field an extra bowler or to lengthen their batting order. The keeper must also be able to stand up to the medium-pace bowlers in the middle overs of a one-day match – a tricky task that was a rarity in days gone by – while limited-overs cricket demands increased fielding ability, with the keeper being expected to chase, intercept and throw just as well as the other infielders. These new demands are in addition to the many existing qualities that the traditional keeper brought to their team.

As well as technical proficiency in the skills of wicketkeeping, there are also many generic tactical, mental and physical qualities that can help keepers fulfil their potential behind the stumps. These are very similar to the qualities displayed by top fielders. This in itself is no surprise, but the keeper may display these qualities in slightly different ways.

SPEED

The ability to move quickly to catch the ball, or to get to the stumps quickly to take the ball, is crucial. Fast feet and the ability to react quickly are also key for a keeper. Thinking quickly and making good decisions that will help speed up their physical response are likewise important if the keeper is to be effective.

AGILITY

An ability to change direction quickly and efficiently is vital. This requires a combination of co-ordination, speed, power and balance. An agile keeper has the ability to make simple, smooth and quick body movements that allow them to move to the ball more efficiently.

CONCENTRATION

The keeper requires an ability to focus on each and every ball and to switch their concentration level up and down between balls. The ability to block out distractions is crucial, particularly when standing up to the wicket.

CO-ORDINATION

It is important to be able to make key parts of the body move in sequence and work together in order to carry out the required catching and fielding skills. Hand-to-eye co-ordination would be an obvious example, especially when related to the keeper's fundamental skill of catching.

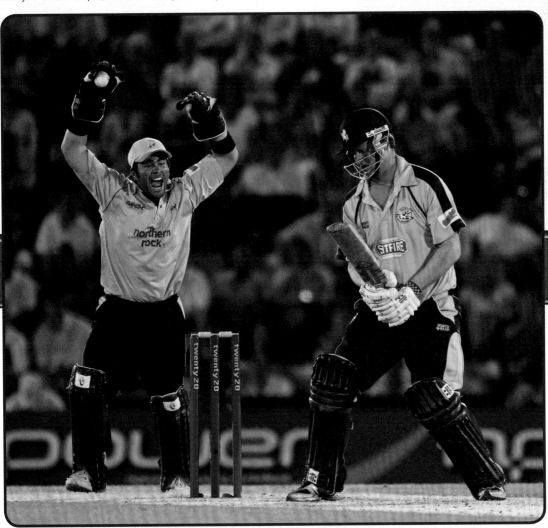

Ben Scott of Middlesex shows co-ordination and concentration to catch Kent's Rob Key

POWER

The need for powerful movements to move the keeper towards the ball quickly is crucial, especially when standing back.

ENDURANCE

The need to be physically and mentally involved in every ball during the innings is taxing, but the keeper needs to be as strong and alert for the last ball of the day as for the first.

DURABILITY

Keepers should be able to withstand the stresses of constant movement up and down into a crouched position, and diving for and catching high-speed deliveries and throws. This can all take its toll on the body and it is important to be physically robust in order to stay in the game. It is also helpful to be mentally durable and therefore able to stand up to the emotional pressures created by the business end of the game. The ability to bounce back from potentially costly dropped catches is essential for the wicketkeeper. Like the goalkeeper in football, the keeper is often in the spotlight, especially when mistakes are made.

SIMPLICITY

The best keepers usually have a very simple technique that allows them to make catching the ball and the art of wicketkeeping look easy.

HARD WORK/SELF-SACRIFICE

Becoming a good keeper requires hard work. Those who want to be the best must be prepared to put in the effort in training, often on their own. Good keepers are always looking to be in the game and must display extra energy at times when the other fielders are flagging. This requires extra hard work and self-sacrifice for the benefit of the team.

POSITIVE BODY LANGUAGE

The best keepers have a presence that is often seen as a positive influence by their fellow fielders, but as an annoyance by the batter. Clever keepers seem to be able to get under the skin of the batter without resorting to 'sledging' and verbal cheap shots. It is also important that the keeper maintains a positive demeanour, as he sets the tone for the fielding side.

LEADERSHIP

Whether or not the keeper is captain of the side they need to show leadership qualities to their fellow team members. Given their prominent and advantageous position on the field, the keeper can also often provide leadership support to the captain.

Sarah Taylor leads the appeal for LBW against New Zealand in the Women's World Cup Final

CAPTAINCY
& COACHING

To the victor the spoils – Charlotte Edwards hugs the Women's World Cup after defeating New Zealand in the 2009 final

ENGLAND CRICKET

INTRODUCTION TO CAPTAINCY

The captain of a cricket team has more responsibility on their shoulders than the captain in almost any other sport. They are often likened to the conductor of an orchestra, ensuring that everyone plays their part in contributing to the overall quality of the performance. One major difference, though, is that unlike a conductor, a cricket captain also has to play an instrument, and play it well.

In addition to performing as a regular player, the captain has many duties to discharge in order to ensure the overall success of the team. This is due mainly to the highly strategic nature of cricket. The constant ebb and flow of a match involves the making of many tactical decisions, and these will have a significant bearing on the game's outcome. During the time that the team is on the field, these decisions are made by the captain.

The captain, therefore, is also effectively the team's coach while it is on the field. Due to the game's regulations, which prevent team coaches from directly influencing play from the sidelines, the captain takes sole responsibility for the decisions that are made. These are generally made in collaboration with the bowler and other key players, but filtering the available information effectively and making decisions that are in the best interests of the team requires a significant level of skill.

Although the role of coaching and the position of head coach has grown in importance in the past decade, the captain still retains a crucial role in the development of teams and players both on and off the field. Effectively the captain and coach have joint responsibility for team management, tactics and performance. The relationship between the captain and coach can at times be a complex one, and potentially problematic if there is a clash of personalities or viewpoints. It is therefore essential for the success of the team that there is a clear philosophy, chain of command and understanding of roles and responsibilities between the two.

In general the coach will tend to take the lead in directing the team off the field, with the captain providing the leadership on the field. The coach and captain must then reach broad agreement on the tactics to be deployed and how they are to be most successfully implemented. At youth and junior levels the coach will have more influence than the captain for obvious reasons, but even at this level the coach will encourage the captain to take as much responsibility as possible in decision-making.

It's not all plain sailing: Hampshire captain Dimi Mascarenhas shows frustration during a championship match against Surrey

ROLE OF THE CAPTAIN

Some of the key tasks involved in being captain are as follows.

SELECTION
At most levels of cricket the captain will be an integral part of the selection process, whereas in most other sports the captain will be in charge of the team that they are given. In cricket, however, the captain has such a crucial role in the deployment of players, particularly the bowlers, that it is important they have confidence in the players who are selected.

THE TOSS
Before a match the teams will toss a coin to decide which team bats first and which bowls. The captain has to rely on lady luck to win them the chance of deciding whether to bat or bowl. The skill involved for the successful captain at the toss is to read the conditions and the make-up of the teams accurately before choosing the option that gives their team the best chance of winning the game.

THE BATTING ORDER
The captain and the coach will tend to agree on the make-up of the batting order prior to the match. This may even be made at the time of selection, when teams are often picked by batting order. There are times, however, when the batting order might be changed by the captain or coach, usually for tactical reasons or as a result of changing conditions.

ENGLAND
CRICKET

DEPLOYMENT OF BOWLERS

One of the most crucial jobs for the captain is to decide who bowls and when. The opening bowlers are usually decided prior to the commencement of the innings or upcoming session of play. After this it is up to the captain to choose when to change the bowling and who should bowl. It is one of the great skills of captaincy to make the right change at the right time. The decision to change the bowling is dependent on many factors and the captain must weigh up all of these before making the decision. The right change is the one that gets the team that vital wicket, or manages to stem the flow of runs.

FIELD PLACEMENT

This is often done in partnership with the bowler. In general terms both captain and bowler should be comfortable with the placement of the fielders. This placing is dependent on many things, including the type of batter, the tactical approach being deployed, the state of the game, the condition of the pitch, and so on. As with bowling changes, the captain must weigh up all these factors when deciding where to place fielders. Sometimes a shrewd change of field placing can be the key to picking up the vital wicket that helps win the game. As a result, the combination of clever bowling changes and shrewd field placing is a major part of the art of captaincy.

DECLARATION AND FOLLOW-ON

In the longer forms of the game, the captain of the batting team may decide to declare their innings closed if they feel that this may help them to win the match. This is usually done when it is believed that the team has scored more than enough runs, but needs the additional time to bowl out the opposition.

The option of the follow-on becomes available to the fielding captain in a two-innings match when the team batting second have failed to get within a reasonable distance of the total scored by the team batting first; this is normally within 150 runs for a three-day match or 200 for a test match. In this instance the captain of the side that has batted first may ask the opposition to bat again, or 'follow-on' from their first innings. This can enable a one-sided match to be completed more quickly.

POWER PLAYS AND REFERRALS

In a one-day international match there are three power plays, one of ten overs at the start of the innings and two further periods of five overs. During this time extra fielding restrictions apply and these change the dynamic of the game significantly. The fielding captain is responsible for deciding when to take one of the five-over power plays and the batting team is able to choose when to take the other. The captain of the batting team will generally be involved in the decision when to take their power play, although he may delegate the decision to the two batters at the crease.

Player referrals are also a recent innovation in the international game. This allows teams to appeal against the decision made by the on-field umpire. This is done by referring the decision to a third 'video' umpire who uses video evidence to review the validity of the decision. The fielding captain is responsible for deciding when to use the referral system on behalf of the fielding team, and the batter at the wicket chooses for the batting team. Each team is usually allowed a maximum of two unsuccessful referrals per innings. It is worth remembering that these playing conditions are experimental and may be subject to change in the future.

DISCIPLINE

The captain is charged with ensuring that both they and their team uphold not only the laws but also the spirit of the game. The captain is ultimately held responsible for team discipline. This is an understated but extremely important part of the captain's role.

Given these many and varied tasks, it is evident that the captain has to have many qualities to do the job well. There is also much more to captaincy than meets the eye. Some players will already possess many of these qualities, but others will need to be learned and developed as a result of experience and intelligent reflection.

Michael Vaughan tosses the coin before the start of a test match against South Africa

QUALITIES OF A CAPTAIN

Justin Langer leads Somerset on to the field at Taunton

Listed in this two-page section are ten of the most important qualities required to make a good captain of a cricket team.

LEADERSHIP

This begins with the ability to imbue the team with strategic and tactical direction. To be able to lead effectively the captain must have the respect of their team-mates and be able to gain their commitment to follow their lead. This tends to be achieved not only by what the captain says, but also by what the captain does, and leading by example is one of the most obvious forms of leadership. The captain should also generate collective responsibility within the team for the fulfilment of its objectives.

ORGANISATION

Most captains have excellent organisational skills. These allow the team and players to see that there is an order and structure to what they are trying to achieve. This helps players to have faith in the captain and makes them more likely to be willing followers. Teams that are organised and have clear plans and objectives tend to be successful.

MOTIVATION

This is a key quality that is defined by the captain's ability to get the best from their team. This is done by gaining the players' commitment to the team's strategic objectives. Different people are motivated by different things and in different ways. It is up to the captain to identify and appeal to the stimuli that make each player want to achieve their best for both themselves and the team.

DISCIPLINE

The captain needs to be disciplined in their behaviour and approach and have the ability to both instil and retain discipline within the team. An ability to stay on task and stick to the plan is crucial to any team's chances of success.

MANAGEMENT

A good captain will have the ability to exercise control over the players under their charge. The ability to manage people effectively and to get the best out of them is a fundamental pillar of good captaincy.

COUNSELLING

At times the captain will need to be 'a shoulder to cry on'. They must be a good listener who can help players recover from a loss of form or crisis of confidence. They must also be able to identify and communicate with players on their level and understand their problems and issues. This ability can help to improve the performance of the players under their charge.

TACTICAL AWARENESS

The ability to read the game tactically and stay one step ahead of the opposition is arguably the greatest on-field quality that any captain can possess. This quality tends to be a combination of intuition and experience. Experience is a difficult quality to find in a young player, but those who are 'scholars' of the game and immerse themselves in its culture at every opportunity tend to learn more quickly.

TOUGHNESS

Sometimes the captain has to be able to make difficult and unpopular decisions in the best interests of the team. They must be able to withstand the pressure to take the easy route when the going gets tough, and to recognise and accept the need for sacrifices.

PASSION AND ENERGY

These are essential qualities if a captain is to establish credibility within the team. A captain who cannot be a motivator and lead by example cannot expect drive and passion from their team when it is most needed. A good captain can motivate their team by their actions, without needing to say a word.

TRUST

The ability to trust and empower players to give of their best and deliver match-winning performances is a powerful quality. Players must likewise be able to trust their captain. A player must have confidence in the soundness of their relationship with their captain if they are to truly give of their best.

England Captain Charlotte Edwards motivates her troops

The late, great Bob Woolmer, pictured in 2006, was generally regarded as the most innovative coach of his generation

ENGLAND CRICKET

HISTORY OF COACHING

Cricket coaching has, like the game itself, evolved greatly in recent times. However, the notion of formal instruction in the techniques of the game, especially to youngsters, has been around for as long as cricket has been involved in the education system. The playing fields of England's private schools became the cradle of cricket coaching, and the 'cream' of England's young men were educated in the finer arts of the noble game. As the Empire spread so did the notion of teaching the techniques of cricket to its colonial population. On reflection this may not have been such a good idea, since the colonials caught on a little too well...

Coaching in cricket was, however, largely restricted to the education of youngsters in the basics of the game. Until about 30 years ago it was generally accepted that once a player became an adult they would be left to their own devices to make the most of their talent. The notion of player improvement was generally left to the captain or senior players. They would help guide and educate younger and less experienced players in the finer points of the game. This model applied from the lowest level of recreational cricket all the way to the pinnacle of the game.

But during the latter part of the 20th century the influence of coaching began to grow, particularly in the professional game. This was probably due to several factors. Firstly, the benefits that coaching was clearly bringing to other sports led to improvements in coach-education programmes in cricket. Secondly, increased revenue coming into the game following the World Series Cricket revolution of the late 1970s made coaches more affordable. And finally, technological advancements made it much easier to analyse performance and provided coaches with more tools to help players develop their game. All of these factors have in their own way created the industry that is modern-day cricket coaching.

The role of the development coach in the game is clear and well-defined in the modern era. The role of the elite coach, however, is less clear, due mainly to the 'curious' nature of the relationship at this level between the captain and the coach. As explained in the section on captaincy, both have a significant influence on the approach that the team takes at different times. This has on occasion led to confusion over who is in overall charge. Some traditionalists feel that the captain should be in charge of the overall direction of the team. This, however, is directly at odds with the growing influence that coaching and coaches have had on performance in recent times. This has the potential to lead to conflict within the team if the coach's and captain's philosophies and methods clash. It is therefore imperative for the success of any team that the coach and captain have a similar outlook on how the game should be played.

The clothing may have changed but the principles remain: England legend Jack Hobbs gives advice to some young batters in 1936

MODERN-DAY COACHING

England coach Andy Flower listens during a team feedback session

There are opportunities for coaches to get involved at every level of the modern game and to work with and have influence on players of all ages and abilities. Traditionally, most coaches tended to get involved in coaching young children in the basics of the game and then progressed to coaching older age-groups as they gained experience. This somewhat narrow path for coaches, however, is changing, with the notion of coaches specialising and becoming experts in particular areas of development rather than 'progressing' up the traditional coaching ladder.

Though the traditional route is still quite rightly seen as a valid career path, there is now much more acceptance and encouragement of 'high-performing' coaches working at all levels of the game. Working with players at different stages of their development undoubtedly involves specialist skill-sets. It is also clear that all coaches possess different attributes and experience that make them better suited to work at one level than another. This specialisation should be encouraged, particularly at the younger levels, as it has the potential to lift the overall standard of play in the long term.

Specialising in coaching children, youths, adults and people with disabilities is becoming much more common, with modern coach education and development programmes now recognising this. As a result, better educational opportunities are being made available for coaches operating in specific development areas. The England and Wales Cricket

Board have invested heavily in the modernisation of coach education and development programmes for this reason, and anyone wishing to get involved in coaching can easily access development opportunities through their local club or via the Internet.

In the past coaches tended to focus heavily on the development of technique, and coach education courses reflected this. Today, however, coaches take a much more holistic approach to the development of players. As a result coaches now look more closely at how they can help players in the four key areas of their development. In addition to having a good technical knowledge coaches must now know how to help players develop tactical awareness and game sense along with their physical and mental skills. All of these skills are required if a player is to fulfil their potential. This applies at whatever level a player performs. So whether it is coaching five-year-olds in a primary school or 25-year-olds in a professional environment, the role of the modern coach is to help their players gain the skills required appropriate to their stage of development.

ECB Pace Bowling Coach Kevin Shine analyses the bowling of Robbie Joseph

Lancashire coach Peter
Moores runs a fielding drill
during pre-match warm-up

ENGLAND
CRICKET

ROLE OF THE COACH

During any coaching session the coach has certain key functions that must be performed well if the session is to meet its objectives and be successful. Every session should be 'player centred', with the needs of the participant at the forefront of the coach's mind at all times. Listed below are some the key roles that a coach performs during a session, with a brief explanation of each.

PLANNING
Any coaching session needs to be well-planned and organised, with a clear plan covering what the participants will be doing, the length of time the session will last, the type of equipment needed, and so on. Coaches also need to be able to forward-plan, in order to ensure that sessions are progressive both for individuals and groups.

SAFETY
The primary concern of the coach at all times should be to ensure that their sessions are as safe as possible. This involves ensuring that the environment and equipment being used are appropriate and in good condition, and that all exercises are planned and carried out in a way that ensures the safety of the participants at all times.

MAKING IT FUN
Irrespective of the level that the coach is working at, it needs to be remembered that people play cricket to enjoy themselves. The coach should never forget this and each session should be fun and enjoyable for all the participants.

EXPLAINING
The coach should be able to clearly explain what they want the participants to do during a session. This should be done in a clear, concise and positive way. This can be greatly aided by putting some thought into the planning of the session.

DEMONSTRATING
The coach should be able to demonstrate the technique that is required from the participants. This can be done by a physical demonstration or by showing images or footage that will help the participants to understand the coach's objective.

PROVIDING AND GENERATING FEEDBACK
What appears to be one of the simplest tasks for a coach is actually the hardest to achieve for many. The ability to give clear and concise feedback is a difficult skill to master, as is the ability to generate feedback through the use of incisive questions. These questions are the key to generating feedback from the players. Feedback is essential if the coach is to really understand a player's needs.

DECISION-MAKING
Coaches must be able to make clear decisions regarding what to do next and be clear in their mind about the path ahead for players or participants. This may involve the coach intervening to help progress the skill being developed or repeating/simplifying the same exercise to help hone the skill. Whichever route is taken, clear decisions on the best way forward are essential for the coach to be successful.

Stuart Broad helps out at a coaching clinic for children in Auckland

SKILLS OF THE COACH

ECB Spin Bowling Coach Mushtaq Ahmed shares some knowledge with Adil Rashid

As discussed in the previous section, the coach has many roles to fulfil when working with players to help improve and develop performance. There are several key skills that the coach must possess if they are to carry out all these roles successfully.

KNOWLEDGE

It is essential that the coach understands and has a sound knowledge of the game. If a coach is to help players learn and improve then they must understand the techniques and tactics that the players will require in order to be successful at the level at which they are playing.

As stated earlier, in addition to sound technical and tactical knowledge, modern-day coaches should also have an understanding of the physical and mental skills which can help their players develop. This knowledge can be gained in many ways. Coach-education courses are designed to help coaches gain the knowledge and competence they require in order to be effective. There are also many informal ways that coaches can improve their understanding of the game, including coaching manuals, DVDs, the Internet and even watching cricket on TV.

COMMUNICATION

This is the most fundamental skill that a coach can possess. All the technical, tactical, physical and mental knowledge is no use unless the coach can effectively communicate it to the players. The ability to

ENGLAND CRICKET

communicate effectively is the greatest challenge for the coach for many reasons. Coaches communicate with players both verbally and non-verbally, and it is important to remember that a coach's actions and deeds say as much as the words that they use. It is also important to remember that communication is a two-way process.

Coaches must be able to give clear and concise information in a way that suits the player's learning needs. Just as important, though, is the ability to create and listen to feedback from the player. This helps to develop the coach's understanding of the players and their needs. Building up a store of 'open questions' which will generate feedback is a good way to develop an effective questioning style. While it is important for coaches to be able to question players effectively, it is also important for them to know when to ask questions and when to be more direct. The simple answer is to adopt whichever method will help to improve performance the most.

TECHNOLOGY

The information technology revolution has transformed the way that coaches can help players learn and improve. At the most basic introductory level this can be as simple as using CD-ROMs and DVDs to demonstrate techniques and tactics to children learning how to play. As players develop and begin to understand their own game, the use of video to analyse performance and help players develop self-awareness

is also an invaluable tool. There are even sports-specific software programs available for coaches working at higher levels, such as Silicon Coach and Quintic, to help provide advanced analysis of cricketing technique.

While coaches can sometimes be hesitant about making use of modern technology, it is important to understand that something as simple as learning to use a video camera is not rocket science, and can help significantly. There is no doubt that the use of IT helps develop performance, and that is why it is important for coaches to embrace it.

ORGANISATION

The ability to be organised and to organise others is fundamental to the success of a coach. Structure is essential if a coach is to help players make systematic progression in their game. Organisation brings with it clear, long-term planning, and this helps to maximise a player's chances of improving and developing their game. The ability to plan and organise coaching sessions also helps to maximise the opportunities for improvement for each player during each session.

Coaches can have all the other key skills they need, including the ability to use technology, possession of excellent communication skills and thorough knowledge of the game, but without the ability to organise well they will never be truly effective. While this may seem to be the least exciting of the skills required its importance should not be under-estimated.

Former England head coach Duncan Fletcher looks on as Pace Bowling Coach Kevin Shine uses a video camera to analyse performance during a net session

OTHER WAYS TO BE INVOLVED

Oval Head Groundsman Bill Gordon rolls the wicket with India's Zaheer Khan looking on

There are many ways other than coaching to either get or stay involved in the game of cricket. Without the many people other than players who participate in the game, cricket simply would not exist. The lifeblood of the game is the thousands of people who volunteer every week to make cricket matches possible. The jobs they do are many and varied, and most do not require any particular experience as a player.

As with playing and coaching, there is a path along which such people can advance and gain experience, which can in turn result in their being recognised and asked to perform their role at a higher level. Cricket therefore provides opportunities for people other than players and coaches to be ambitious and to achieve success in their chosen field. However, the majority of people who get involved do so purely to help out their local club and community. These are the people who make the game tick.

OFFICIALS

The role of umpires and scorers was covered in the first section of this manual. The need for officials to oversee the fair playing of a match is fundamental to everything that cricket stands for. People in the UK or Europe who wish to become a match official, whether an umpire or a scorer, can do so by contacting their local club and/or by contacting the Association of Cricket Officials, or ECB ACO as it is more commonly known. A link to this organisation can be found through the ECB website at www.ecb.co.uk.

ADMINISTRATORS

Cricket is a sport that needs to be well-administered. As a team sport, it is played by clubs which run well when people give up their time to do jobs that make sure all is properly organised. As described earlier, the facilities required for a cricket match are quite specialist and their preparation and upkeep is essential for a cricket club to function. Like clubs in many other sports, cricket clubs need presidents to oversee their running, secretaries to deal with correspondence and paperwork, treasurers to look after the money and various other people to make up the committees that ensure their affairs run smoothly.

The leagues and associations that organise groups of clubs also require administrators, and many successful club officials are asked to step up and carry out administrative duties at this higher level. This creates a pathway for administrators who excel to rise all the way to the sport's regional, national and even world governing bodies.

People who are interested in getting involved and putting their administrative skills to good use should contact their local club in the first instance to express their interest.

ECB Chief Executive David Collier and Chairman Giles Clarke during a press conference

GROUND STAFF

A significant amount of work is required to prepare the wicket and field that make a game of cricket possible. There is a particular art in the preparation of a pitch for a cricket match, ideally involving it being cut and rolled, covered and watered when necessary, and having the lines properly marked on it. This is in addition to making sure that the outfield is of sufficient quality for the ball to roll as true as is possible. A well-tended cricket ground in summer is indeed a beautiful sight, and knowledgeable and hard-working groundsmen are worth their weight in gold. People interested in getting involved in ground maintenance can learn the ropes through courses run by the Institute of Groundsmanship, or IOG. See their website at www.iog.org.

BEHIND THE SCENES

ECB Pace Bowling Coach Kevin Shine pictured with players and coaches from the Young Elite Bowling Programme outside the National Cricket Performance Centre at Loughborough

THE NATIONAL CRICKET PERFORMANCE CENTRE

The ECB opened what was then called the National Academy at Loughborough University in October 2003, when it was officially opened by Her Majesty the Queen. The inauguration of this state-of-the-art facility marked a major step forward for cricket in England and Wales. It was renamed the National Cricket Performance Centre (NCPC) in June 2007.

The NCPC, however, is more than just a training centre for the England team, as it caters for all of England's performance programmes including men, women, under-age and disability squads. The indoor facility is the largest purpose-built indoor training facility in world cricket. The campus at Loughborough also boasts a top-quality outdoor cricket ground and net facilities.

ENGLAND
CRICKET

England
performance
programme
players hold
a morning
meeting prior
to a training
session

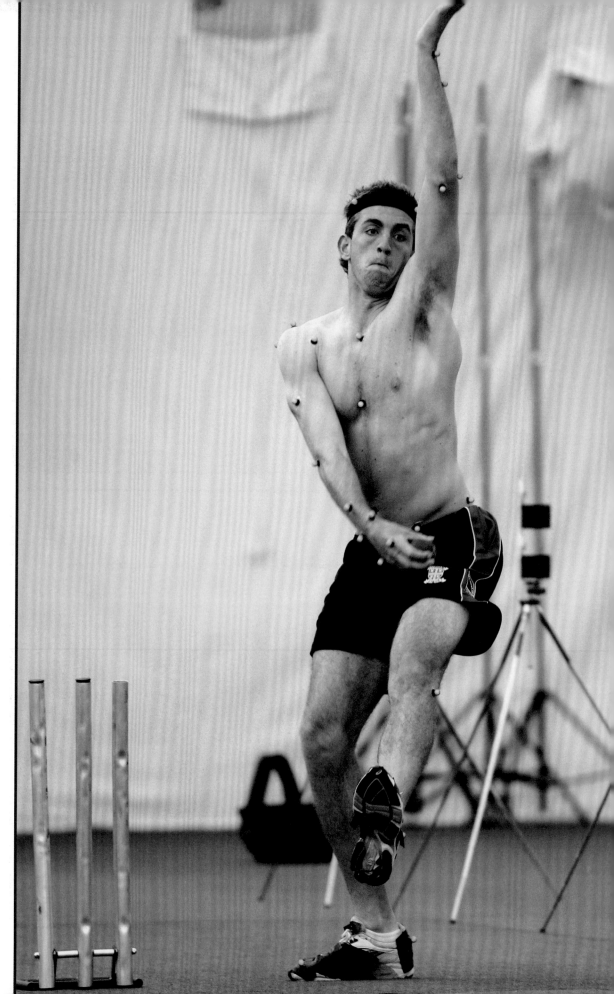

Liam Plunkett
bowls with
reflective
markers during
a biometric
calibration
session

ENGLAND
CRICKET

Former
England fast
bowling coach
Troy Cooley
uses a laptop
computer
to analyse
performance
during
biometric
testing

ECB Information
Manager David
Rose uses
IT to analyse
performance
during an
England
performance
programme
training session

England's under-19 players during a fielding training session in preparation for a winter tour to South Africa

England bowler Laura Marsh and Assistant Coach Jack Birkenshaw discuss tactics during a training session at the outdoor nets

ENGLAND
CRICKET

Jade Dernbach
takes part in
a speed test
during the ECB
Young Elite
Fast Bowler
Programme

The England
performance
programme
players during a
practice session
using bowling
machines

GLOSSARY

ACO – Association of Cricket Officials.

APPEAL – When the fielding side shouts 'Howzat!' as a request to the umpire to declare a batter out.

ARM BALL – A variation delivery used by a finger-spin bowler which, rather than spinning sideways off the pitch, goes straight on with the arm.

ASHES – The contents of a small urn that has become the trophy for the winners of the biennial test match series between England and Australia.

BACK DEFENSIVE – A defensive stroke played by a batter following a movement on to the back foot.

BACK-FOOT DRIVE – An attacking stroke played by a batter following a movement on to the back foot.

BAT-PAD CATCHER – A fielding position close to the wicket whose principal aim is to catch a ball rebounding from the bat or bat and pad.

BEAMER – A dangerous delivery by a bowler that is normally directed towards the batter's head without bouncing.

BODYLINE SERIES – An infamous series played between Australia and England in 1932–3 when England were generally felt to have used unsportsmanlike tactics. The England bowlers were instructed to target the ball consistently towards the head and body of the Australian batsmen. This breached the spirit of the game if not the laws at the time.

BOUNCER – A fast short-pitched delivery by a pace bowler, designed to rise to around shoulder- or head-height of the batter.

BOUNDARY – The edge of the playing area, normally marked by a rope or white line. The term is also used when the batter hits the ball over or past the boundary, when they are termed to have hit a 'boundary'.

BYE – The name given to a run or runs scored when the ball has not hit the bat or batter.

CHINAMAN – The standard type of delivery by a left-arm wrist-spin bowler which spins from left to right after pitching.

COVER – A key fielding position on the off side of the wicket whose main aim is to stop a run being scored.

COVER DRIVE – A front-foot attacking stroke played by the batter with the ball travelling past or over the cover fielding position.

CREASE – The white line markings at either end of the wicket which regulate where the stumps are placed, where the batter stands and where the bowler delivers from.

DEEP – The area of the cricket field furthest away from the wicket and near the boundary.

DELIVERY – The term given to a ball bowled at the batter. Each bowler bowls six fair deliveries at a time. This constitutes an over.

DOOSRA – An unorthodox delivery bowled by a finger spinner which spins in the opposite direction to their normal delivery.

DUSTBOWL – A term applied to a playing surface that is overly dry and dusty.

ECB – England and Wales Cricket Board.

FAST BOWLING – A classification given to deliveries that are bowled much quicker than what is generally regarded as the norm.

FAST WICKET – A generally hard playing surface that encourages the ball to retain most of its pace after bouncing.

FINE LEG – A fielding position behind the wicket on the leg side close to the boundary.

FINGER SPIN – A classification applied to bowlers who spin the ball principally by using the energy created by their fingers.

FIRST-CLASS CRICKET – The term applied to test cricket and the highest level of domestic cricket played in any of the ten test-playing nations (Australia, Bangladesh, England, India, New Zealand, Pakistan, South Africa, Sri Lanka, West Indies and Zimbabwe).

FLIPPER – An unorthodox delivery bowled by a wrist spinner which 'flips' out underneath the hand as the ball is released.

FOLLOW-ON – A condition that can be enforced on a team batting second who have not achieved a total (as pre-agreed) close enough to that of the team which batted first in a two-innings match. The captain of the team that batted first may ask the team batting

second to 'follow on' – to bat again –
in order to try and dismiss them for a
second time before the combined
score of their two innings passes that of
the team which batted first.

FORWARD DEFENSIVE – A
defensive stroke played by a batter
following a movement on to the front
foot.

FRONT-FOOT DRIVE – An
attacking stroke played by a batter
following a movement on to the front
foot.

FULL TOSS – A delivery by the
bowler which reaches the batter
without bouncing.

GLIDE – Description of a stroke
played by a batter which glances or
deflects the ball rather than powerfully
striking it.

GOOGLY – An unorthodox delivery
by a wrist spin bowler which spins the
ball in the opposite direction to their
standard delivery.

GREEN WICKET – The term
applied to a playing surface which
generally favours the bowlers due to a
higher moisture content than normal.
So called due to its greener-than-
normal colouring.

GUARD – The position a batter takes
at the wicket in relation to the stumps.
For example, in the batter's normal
stance a 'leg-stump guard' would place
the bat in front of the leg stump.

GULLY – A fielding position close to
the wicket behind the batter on the off
side of the field.

HALF VOLLEY – A delivery by the
bowler which allows the batter to move
towards it and make contact just after
the ball pitches.

HOOK SHOT – An attacking cross-
bat shot played to a fast short-pitched
ball which has bounced to around
shoulder or head height. The ball is
generally hit on the leg side behind the
wicket.

ICC – International Cricket Council.

IN-OUT FIELD – A term given to a
tactical field placing which consists of
an even combination of attacking and
defensive field positions.

IN-SWINGER – A delivery by the
bowler which curves in the air towards
the batter.

INFIELDER – A term given to
players fielding within a distance of
approximately 30yds of the bat.

INNINGS – The name applied to the
time for which a team bats. An innings
will last until either all ten wickets have
been lost by the batting team or until
the pre-agreed number of overs has
been bowled.

INTER-CRICKET – A modified
form of the game designed for
teenagers, using a semi-soft ball and
lighter-than-standard protective
equipment.

IPL – Indian Premier League.

KWIK CRICKET – A modified form
of the game designed for children and
beginners, played with plastic
equipment and a soft ball.

LATE CUT – An attacking cross-bat
stroke which is hit behind the wicket on
the off side.

LBW (LEG BEFORE WICKET)
A method of dismissal when the batter
is adjudged out if the ball strikes their
leg when it would have gone on to hit
the wicket.

LEG BREAK – The standard
delivery bowled by a wrist-spin bowler.

LEG BYE – The name given to a run
or runs scored when a ball has hit the
batter rather than the bat.

LEG CUTTER – A delivery bowled
by a pace bowler which involves
cutting the fingers across the seam
towards the body as the ball is
released.

LEG GLANCE – A stroke by the
batter which deflects the ball behind
the wicket on the leg side.

LEG-SIDE FIELD – A fielding
configuration which has the majority
of the fielders on the leg side of the
wicket.

LEG SPINNER – A term used to
describe both a wrist-spin bowler and
the standard delivery that they bowl.

LEG STUMP – The inside stump of
the three that make up the wicket, the
one which is generally closest to the
batter's legs.

LENGTH OF DELIVERY – This
refers to the distance to which the ball
is pitched by the bowler in relation to
the wicket and the batter: eg, 'good
length', 'full length', etc.

LIMITED-OVERS CRICKET – A form of the game which limits the maximum number of overs bowled by each side.

LINE OF DELIVERY – This refers to the direction of a bowled ball as measured against an imaginary line drawn along the length of the pitch. For example, a 'leg stump line' would be aimed in the general direction of the batter's leg stump.

LOFTED DRIVE – A front-foot attacking shot where the ball is hit in the air.

LONG HOP – A slow short-pitched delivery which is generally regarded as being of poor quality.

MCC – Marylebone Cricket Club.

MID-OFF – A fielding position in front of the batter on the off side of the wicket whose purpose is to stop a run being scored.

MID-ON – A fielding position in front of the batter on the on/leg side of the wicket whose main aim is to stop a run being scored.

MID-WICKET – A key fielding position on the leg side of the wicket whose purpose is to stop a run being scored.

NCPC – National Cricket Performance Centre at Loughborough.

NO BALL – An illegal delivery by a bowler which is usually due to their foot landing in a position outside the allowed area.

ODI – A One-Day International match or series of matches which are played between the top 16 cricketing nations.

OFF BREAK – The standard delivery bowled by a finger-spin bowler.

OFF CUTTER – A delivery bowled by a pace bowler which involves cutting the fingers across the seam away from the body as the ball is released.

OFF DRIVE – A front-foot attacking stroke played by the batter with the ball travelling past or over the mid-off fielding position.

OFF-SIDE FIELD – A fielding configuration which has the majority of the fielders on the off side of the wicket.

OFF STUMP – The outside stump of the three that make up the wicket, the one which is generally furthest away from the batter's legs.

ON DRIVE – A front-foot attacking stroke played by the batter with the ball travelling past or over the mid-on fielding position.

OUTFIELDER – The term used to describe players fielding close to the boundary.

OUT-SWINGER – A delivery by the bowler which curves in the air away from the batter.

OVER – A set of six consecutive deliveries bowled from one end of the wicket.

PACE BOWLING – A general classification given to deliveries that are either fast or medium-fast. The term tends to be applied to all categories of bowling other than spin.

POINT – A key fielding position square of the wicket on the off side whose purpose is to stop a run being scored.

POPPING CREASE – The front line of the crease markings, used to adjudge run-outs and stumpings.

POWER PLAY – A period of overs in a limited-overs match which restricts the number of fielders allowed in the deep. This playing condition was introduced to encourage attacking batting.

PULL SHOT – An attacking cross-bat shot to a short-pitched delivery which is hit on the leg side of the wicket.

REFERRAL – Used in televised matches, the on-field umpire may refer certain decisions to a third umpire who may use video evidence to assist the umpires in making decisions.

RETURN CREASE – The side lines of the crease markings which are generally used to regulate the position of the bowler during the delivery, ensuring that they bowl relatively close to the stumps.

REVERSE SWING – A concept whereby the ball curves in the air in the opposite direction to conventional swing.

RUN-OUT – A form of dismissal where the batter is adjudged out after failing to make their ground behind the popping crease when attempting a run.

SEAM BOWLING – A sub-classification of pace bowling where the

ENGLAND
CRICKET

bowler specialises in landing the ball on the seam, causing lateral deviation.

SEAMER – The name given to a pace bowler who specialises in landing the ball on the seam to cause lateral deviation.

SHORT LEG – A fielding position close to the wicket on the leg side of the bat, also known as a 'bat pad' fielder.

SILLY – A term which prefixes some fielding position when moved very close to the bat.

SILLY POINT – A fielding position close to the wicket on the off side of the bat, also known as a 'bat pad' fielder.

SKIM CATCH – A catch defined by a fast-travelling ball hit to an infielder with a flat trajectory.

SLIP – A close catching position behind the wicket close to the wicketkeeper whose principle aim is to catch a ball that glances from the edge of the bat.

SLOW WICKET – A playing surface which is usually softer than normal and encourages the ball to decelerate more than usual after pitching,

SPIN BOWLING – A classification of bowling in which the bowler specialises in imparting spin on the ball, using the fingers and/or wrist to achieve lateral deviation of the pitch.

SQUARE CUT – A cross-bat attacking stroke played to a wide short-pitched ball square of the wicket on the off side.

SQUARE LEG – A fielding position square of the wicket on the leg side whose main purpose is to save a run.

STANFORD SERIES – A series of Twenty20 matches sponsored by Sir Allen Stanford and played in Antigua in 2008.

STRAIGHT DRIVE – An attacking front-foot shot where the ball travels straight back past or over the bowler.

STUMPED – A form of dismissal which involves the wicketkeeper catching the ball and removing the bails while the batter is out of their ground in front of the popping crease.

SWEEP SHOT – A cross-bat attacking shot generally played on or behind square on the leg side of the wicket

SWEEPER – A term given to any fielder who is fielding in the deep and defending the boundary.

SWING BOWLING – A sub-classification of pace bowling where the bowler specialises in curving the ball in the air both in and away from the batter.

SWITCH HIT – An attacking shot where the batter reverses their stance to execute the stroke.

T20 (TWENTY 20 CRICKET) A limited-overs match in which each team may bat for a maximum of 20 overs

TAPEBALL – An informal variation of the game played with a taped-up tennis ball to increase the pace of the

ball. It originated and is played principally in the Indian sub-continent, particularly in Pakistan.

TEST-MATCH CRICKET – The highest form of the game. Matches are played over a maximum of five days between the established top ten nations in world cricket (see 'First-class cricket').

THIRD MAN – A fielding position close to the boundary behind the wicket on the off side of the field.

TOP SPINNER – A variation in a spin bowler's armoury which features over spin rather than side spin.

WICKET – This term can be applied both to the sets of stumps at either end of the pitch and to the playing surface between the stumps. A 'wicket' is also deemed to be lost if a batter is dismissed.

WIDE BALL – An illegal delivery which is bowled so wide of the wicket that the batter is deemed unable to make contact.

WRIST SPIN – A classification of bowler who spins the ball principally by using the energy created by the wrist.

YORKER – A delivery normally bowled by a fast bowler which pitches very close to the batter's feet or the stumps.

CLUBS AND SCHOOLS

MEASURE YOURSELVES LIKE THE PROFESSIONALS

CRICKET **CLUBS** AND **SCHOOLS** ACROSS THE WORLD CAN SIGN UP FOR THE **PROFESSIONAL MVP TREATMENT**

No more arguing about who's the best player on your team. All your scorecard information will be processed to determine who is grinding out the match winning performances ...and who is full of hot air!

The MVP's are based on a cumulative points system, rewarding all valued elements that are imperative to win cricket matches.

Runs, strike rates, wickets, economy rates and catches, all in one formula = MVP.

Find out more at **www.mycricketmvp.com**